The Essential
Louisiana Seafood
COOKBOOK

Recipes by **Stanley Dry** *with Photography & Styling by* **Eugenia Uhl**

A Renaissance Publishing Production
Copyright 2016 Renaissance Publishing, LLC
Copyright 2016 Stanley Dry
Copyright 2016 Eugenia Uhl

All rights reserved, including the right of reproduction in whole or in part in any form.

Author: Stanley Dry
Photographer: Eugenia Uhl
Editor: Melanie Warner Spencer
Art Director: Sarah George
Chief Executive Officer: Todd Matherne
President: Alan Campell
Executive Vice President: Errol Laborde
Printed in USA

ISBN 978-0-9977436-0-9

The Essential Louisiana Seafood Cookbook™ was produced by Renaissance Publishing, LLC 110 Veterans Memorial Blvd., Suite 123 Metairie, LA 70005.
MyNewOrleans.com
LouisianaLife.com

A locally-owned and operated company, Renaissance Publishing produces myriad award-winning city and regional lifestyle and luxury magazines, including *New Orleans Magazine*, *Biz New Orleans*, *New Orleans Homes & Lifestyles*, *Louisiana Life*, *Acadiana Profile*, *St. Charles Avenue* and *New Orleans Bride*, as well as various custom and niche publications.

Set in Adobe Caslon

"Nature has been exceptionally kind to the Louisiana cook...Fresh- and salt-water fish, shrimp, oysters, crabs, crayfish, turtles and frogs are plentiful and cheap... In the preparation of sea food Creole cuisine is at its best. Mark Twain spoke of the pompano cooked in Louisiana as being 'delicious as the less criminal forms of sin,' and Thackeray and Irvin S. Cobb found New Orleans *bouillabaisse* unexcelled."

Federal Writers' Project,
"Louisiana: A Guide to the State," 1941

Contents

7 Editor's Note
8 Author's Note

Salads & Appetizers

13 Artichoke Hearts, Green Peas & Lump Crabmeat
15 Crawfish with White Wine, Lemon & Capers
17 Crawfish, Avocado & Quinoa Salad
19 Avocados Stuffed with Shrimp
21 Crab Salad
23 Artichokes Stuffed with Shrimp
25 Crawfish with Olive Salad & Orzo
27 Shrimp & Couscous Salad
29 Marinated Crab Claws

Gumbos & Soups

33 Shrimp & Okra Gumbo Light
35 Shrimp, Andouille & Okra Gumbo
37 Shrimp, Oyster & Crabmeat Gumbo
39 Duck, Andouille & Oyster Gumbo
41 Shrimp Filé Gumbo
43 Dried Shrimp & Tasso Gumbo with Poached Eggs
45 Green Redfish Soup
47 Navy Bean, Andouille & Shrimp Soup
49 Saffron Seafood Soup
51 Swordfish, Tasso & Potato Soup

Etouffées & Stews

55 Crawfish and Eggplant Stew
57 Quick Crawfish Stew
59 Crawfish Stew Light
61 30-Minute Crawfish Etouffée
63 Crawfish Piquante with Rice Waffles
65 Shrimp Creole Light
67 Shrimp & Lump Crabmeat Etouffée with Cornmeal Waffles
69 Shrimp & Pork Stew
71 Shrimp & Egg Stew
73 Courtbouillion

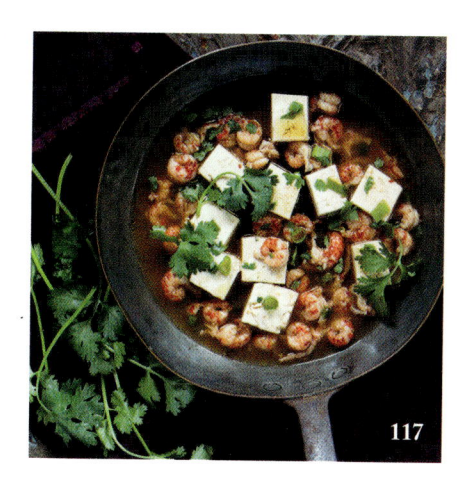

Jambalayas & Rice

77 Crawfish Fried Rice

79 Crawfish & Tasso Jambalaya

81 Shrimp & Ham Jambalaya

83 Shrimp & Mirliton Rice Dressing

Pan Fried, Grilled, Broiled & Boiled

87 Stir-Fried Crawfish with Tasso & Bok Choy

89 Boiled Crabs

91 Broiled Catfish

93 Crab Cakes with Lemon Mayonnaise

95 Fried Catfish

97 Gulf Fish with Crabmeat

99 Pecan Crusted Trout

101 Carpetbag Steak

103 Venison with Italian Sausage & Oysters

105 Shrimp Cakes

Lagniappe

109 Crawfish with Red Sauce & Spaghetti

111 Crawfish Omelet with Penne & Green Peas

113 Baked Tomatoes Filled with Crabmeat

115 Spicy Crawfish Spread

117 Spicy Tofu with Crawfish

119 Mini Crawfish Pies

121 Crawfish Tacos

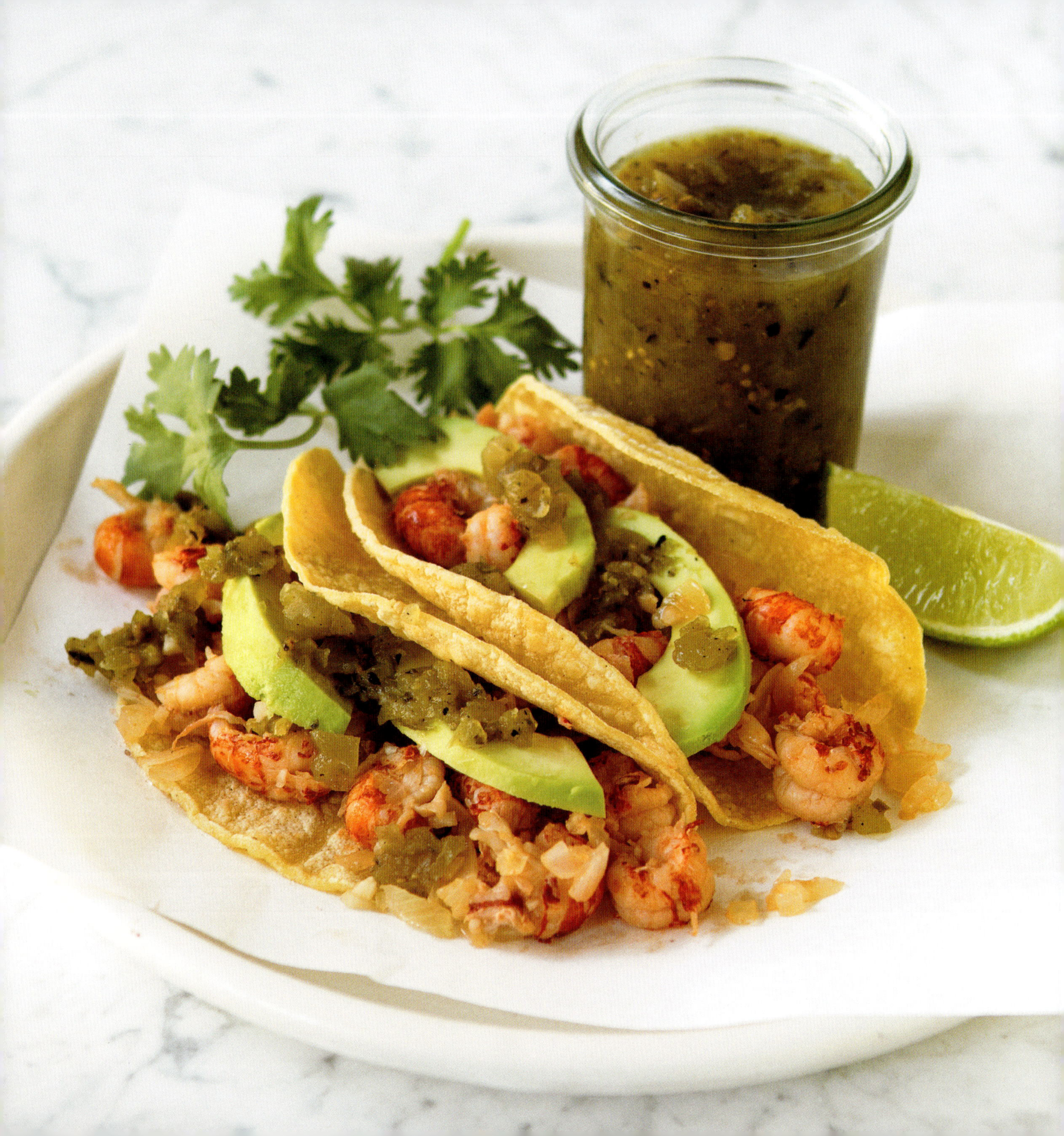

Editor's Note

Seafood wasn't a big part of my culinary upbringing. The first 30 years of my life were spent as a landlocked Kentuckian living half time on a cattle farm and the other half in the city. We were meat and potatoes people and when seafood did show up on our dinner plates, the usual suspects were classic shrimp cocktail, crab legs or lobster tail at a white tablecloth establishment during formal family celebrations. The occasional fried oyster plate at my grandfather's favorite seafood dive on the Ohio River was a welcome treat, too. Which is why living in Louisiana — with its vast seafood traditions — is for me a revelation. Seafood in Louisiana isn't a special occasion food. Rather, it's a staple in every home cook and professional chef's kitchen. Which made it quite a project narrowing down the collection of recipes for this book.

"The Essential Louisiana Seafood Cookbook" is a sequel of sorts to "The Essential Louisiana Cookbook," published in 2014 and now in its second printing. For each volume, I worked with author Stanley Dry, *Louisiana Life* "Kitchen Gourmet" columnist and former senior editor of *Food & Wine* magazine. In addition to being a writer and editor who knows his way around the page, Dry is an accomplished cook who knows his way around the kitchen. The concept of each book was to curate the best of Dry's "Kitchen Gourmet" recipes, but as is so often the case, the reality was a bit different and more involved than the theory. We did bring together Dry's best recipes, but he updated and tweaked many of the offerings to ensure the tastiest, most au courant version of each dish. Dry's recipes are simple and rely upon fresh, local, seasonal ingredients, pulling together the best fruits of the region. In this volume, we get those elements, coupled with the best fruits of the state's waterways from the Gulf Coast to the lakes, streams and, of course, Cajun crawfish farms.

We teamed up again with New Orleans photographer Eugenia Uhl, whose work has appeared in *Louisiana Life*, *New Orleans Magazine*, *Southern Accents*, *Metropolitan Home*, *GQ Magazine* and *Travel & Leisure*. In addition to photographing the mouth-watering images in "The Essential Louisiana Cookbook" and this beautiful book, Uhl's other cookbook credits include "Commander's Kitchen" for Commander's Palace and "New Orleans Home Cooking" by Dale Curry, Pelican Publishing.

Art Director Sarah George played upon the simple design of the first book, somehow finding an even more minimalistic presentation. The clean, modern design highlights each recipe and companion image, drawing in the viewer or reader and leaving them wanting more.

This cookbook was created by an award-winning team of writers, artists and Louisianians who love to cook, photograph, write about, read about, talk about and eat the abundant culinary offerings of this region. The first book became a staple in my own kitchen. I return to it time and time again for meals that are now tried-and-true favorites. I look forward to further exploring Dry's new and traditional ways of preparing the myriad seafood offerings of Louisiana. I'm confident that soon, not only will there be another favorite in my cookbook library, but that you too will find a new beloved collection in "The Essential Louisiana Seafood Cookbook."

— *Melanie Warner Spencer*

Author's Note

When one thinks about Louisiana cooking, the first thing that comes to mind is seafood. And for good reason. Graced as we are, with an abundance of riches from the Gulf, as well as from our marshes, swamps, lakes and bayous, we are in an enviable position compared to landlocked areas where supplies are limited, at best. Over centuries, the practitioners of our cuisine, both professional chefs and home cooks, have perfected the art of cooking seafood.

In addition to its gustatory delights, seafood is a vital segment of the Louisiana economy. One out of every 70 jobs is related to the seafood industry, which has an annual economic impact of over $2.4 billion. Shrimp, crabs, oysters, crawfish, various species of fin-fish, caviar, frogs and alligators are important both on the table and on the balance sheet.

Shrimping constitutes the largest segment of our seafood industry. Since Louisiana lands about a third of the country's total catch, it's no wonder we have so many ways to cook and serve this delicious crustacean. Boiled shrimp, fried shrimp, shrimp remoulade, shrimp gumbos, stews, poor boys and jambalayas are emblematic of both Cajun and Creole cuisines, but those dishes only scratch the surface of shrimp cookery.

Shrimp is a most cooperative ingredient, quite comfortable with a wide variety of companions. Shrimp's natural sweetness can be accentuated with onions or thrown into relief with the addition of lemon or horseradish. Shrimp are equally at home with butter or olive oil, with mild flavors or strong ones. Given its ability to forge alliances, a shrimp would be an unbeatable candidate in the political world.

Before the age of refrigeration, dried shrimp constituted a significant industry in Louisiana. Dried shrimp are still produced here on a small scale and are readily available in grocery stores. They are popular as a snack and are also used in some dishes, such as a gumbo of dried shrimp and eggs, for the intensity of flavor they impart.

It's difficult to imagine an environment more perfect for the blue crab than Louisiana's jagged coast, which nestles an abundance of marshes and estuaries within some 7,721 miles of shoreline. Blue crabs are found along the East Coast and across the Gulf states from Florida to Texas. Louisiana landings account for 83 percent of the Gulf total and 25 percent of the United States total.

The blue crab is an irascible beast with a fearsome demeanor that belies its inner beauty. Only its scientific name, "Callinectes sapidus" (tasty beautiful swimmer), gives a hint of how sweet and succulent is the meat inside that hard shell. What a job it is to extract the snowy white deliciousness, but what a joy it is to savor it. From spicy boiled crabs spread out on newspaper-covered tables and accompanied by cold bottles of beer to delicate lumps of snow-white crabmeat served in elegant restaurants along with expensive bottles of Champagne or chardonnay, the blue crab's appeal is near universal.

Of all the glorious seafood that comes from the Gulf, in addition to shrimp and crabs, oysters are at the very top of my list. As far as I'm concerned, the abundance of those three is reason enough for living in Louisiana. I can't think of many meals I'd rather eat than a couple dozen oysters on the half shell followed by a plate of fried oysters.

And I'm not alone on that score. "The Picayune's Creole Cook Book," published in 1900, observed that, "Everyone who has visited New Orleans in winter has noted the exceptionally palatable oysters that are sold in every restaurant and by numerous small vendors on almost every other corner or so throughout the lower section of the city. In the cafés, the hotels, the oyster saloons, they are served in every conceivable style known to epicures and caterers." Not much has changed in the last 100 years.

Crawfish have become as much a symbol of Louisiana as anything I can think of. Observers noted the availability of crawfish in New Orleans markets at least as early as 1803, but the first recorded commercial harvest was in 1880, when 23,400 pounds were harvested from the Atchafalaya Basin. Compare that to today, when the annual crawfish harvest is 110 million pounds.

Author's Note

Since crawfish have a long and storied history in French cuisine, it was only natural that settlers from France should have warmly embraced the native supply. Consequently, crawfish dishes occupied places of prominence in the Creole cuisine of New Orleans. Recipes for a variety of crawfish dishes appeared in two of the earliest Louisiana cookbooks, "Mme. Begue and Her Recipes" and "The Picayune's Creole Cook Book."

Acadian refugees who settled in Louisiana had neither the money nor the background of wealthy New Orleans Creoles. Certainly they had no tradition of eating crawfish nor did they have a repertoire of crawfish dishes, as did the French. According to historian Carl A. Brasseaux, crawfish did not play a significant role in the diet of the Cajuns. Even in the early 20th century, about the only time Cajuns ate crawfish was during Lent, when they boiled the crustaceans.

The year 1959 is often cited as the time when the fortunes of the crawfish began to change. That was the year the Louisiana Legislature named Breaux Bridge the Crawfish Capital of the World and allocated funds for research into crawfish farming. The town celebrated its centennial anniversary that year with a festival that, the following year, officially became the Crawfish Festival. During the 1960s, crawfish farming expanded greatly and entrepreneurs opened crawfish processing plants to peel and package crawfish tails for restaurant and home consumption.

The growth of crawfish farming in South Louisiana both increased the supply of the crustacean and extended the season. At the same time, the Crawfish Festival helped to raise the image of crawfish and popularize its consumption. With a steady supply of peeled crawfish tails that could be frozen for the off-season, restaurant chefs and home cooks were encouraged to expand their use of crawfish. Today, crawfish are found in a dizzying variety of preparations.

Of all the creations that the late, great Louisiana Chef Paul Prudhomme introduced to the dining public, none is more associated with his name than blackened redfish. And it was blackened redfish that led, in part, to the appearance of fish species that had largely been absent from Louisiana menus.

The blackened redfish craze reached such proportions in the eighties — not just in Louisiana, but nationally — that redfish came dangerously close to being wiped out by commercial fishermen who used spotter planes to locate and harvest huge schools of fish. The state was slow to act, but finally a ban was imposed and other species began appearing on menus. Some of those newcomers had been known colloquially as "trash fish." Since the fish were delicious in their own right, this was not only unfair, but it was also a poor marketing label, so the term "underutilized species" came into vogue.

The upshot has been that menus and fish markets now boast a much larger variety of fish than in the past. In addition to trout, snapper, redfish, flounder, pompano and catfish, diners are likely to encounter mahi-mahi, black drum, tuna, salmon, swordfish, hake, sheepshead, grouper and others.

The recipes in this book, which were originally published in *Louisiana Life* magazine, range from fairly traditional versions to more contemporary interpretations, although it should be said that even traditional dishes can vary greatly from one cook to another. To my mind, all the variations in recipes that go by the same name are merely indicative of the free form, improvisational nature of Louisiana cooking. Certainly there are parallels between our food and our music. Our food evolved from the hands and minds of cooks, not from books, just as jazz, as well as Cajun and zydeco music, evolved from the creativity of musicians, not from sheet music. And all of them are still evolving.

The emphasis in these recipes is on using Louisiana seafood and quality local ingredients. Wherever possible, without compromising the integrity of the dish, techniques and methods have been simplified to make the recipes doable for the average person. We have a variety of acceptable timesaving ingredients (such as bottled roux and commercial chicken broth) at our disposal, and I see no reason why we shouldn't use them.

— *Stanley Dry*

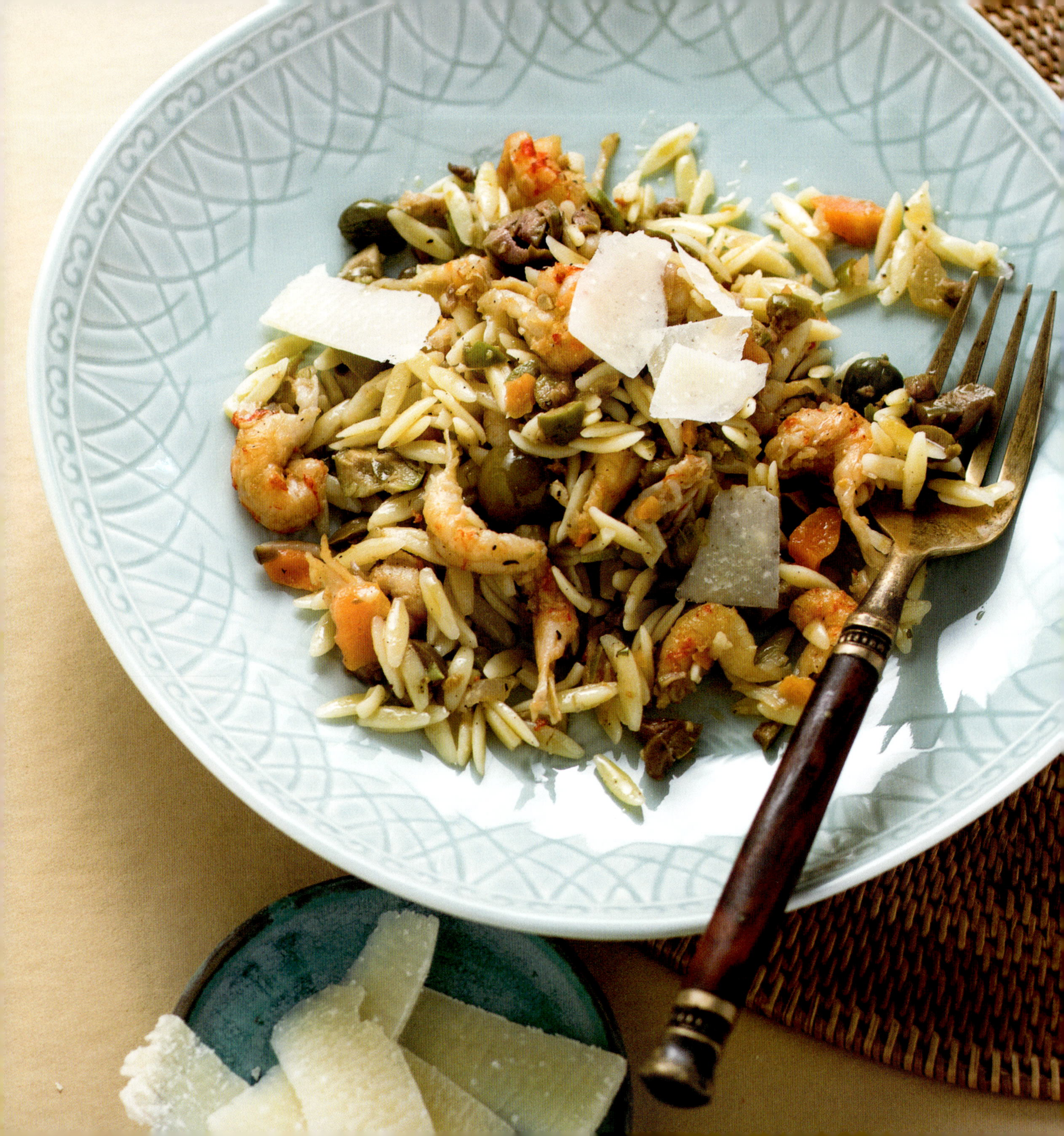

Salads & Appetizers

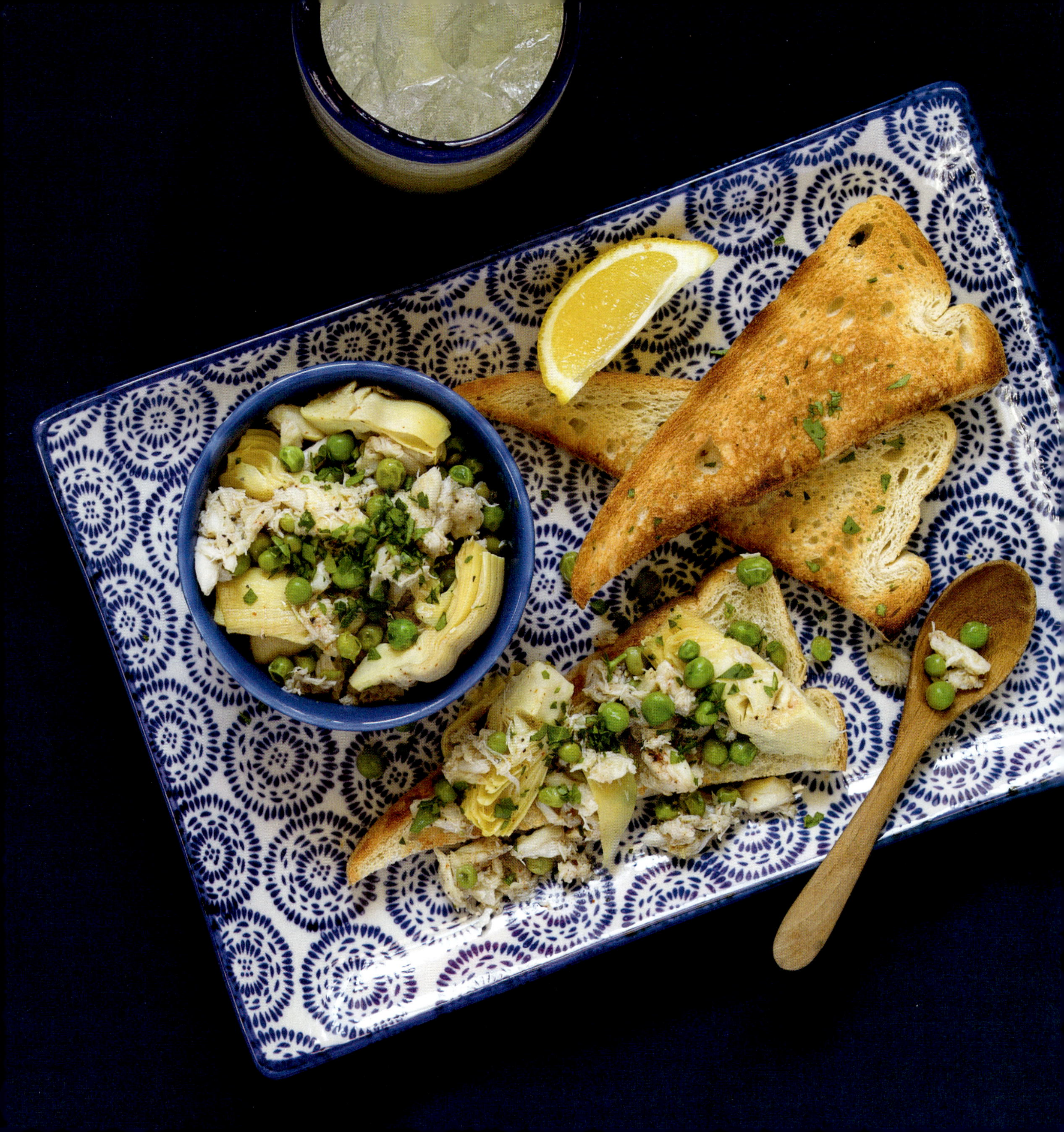

Artichoke Hearts, Green Peas & Lump Crabmeat

....

This is a very quick dish to prepare. It can serve as the centerpiece of a luncheon or as first course in a dinner menu.

1	(9 oz.) package frozen artichoke hearts
2	tablespoons extra-virgin olive oil
¼	cup dry white wine
1	tablespoon freshly squeezed lemon juice
1	cup frozen green peas
1	pound lump crabmeat, picked over
	Coarse salt & freshly ground black pepper
	Cayenne
2	tablespoons chopped parsley
4	slices toasted bread

Combine artichoke hearts, olive oil, wine and lemon juice in a large non-reactive skillet. Bring to a boil, cover and cook for 2 minutes. Add green peas, stir, cover and cook until artichoke hearts are tender, about 3 minutes. Add crabmeat and stir gently so as not to break up lumps. Season to taste with salt and peppers. Cook just until crabmeat is heated through. Sprinkle with chopped parsley and serve on toasted bread.

Makes 4 servings.

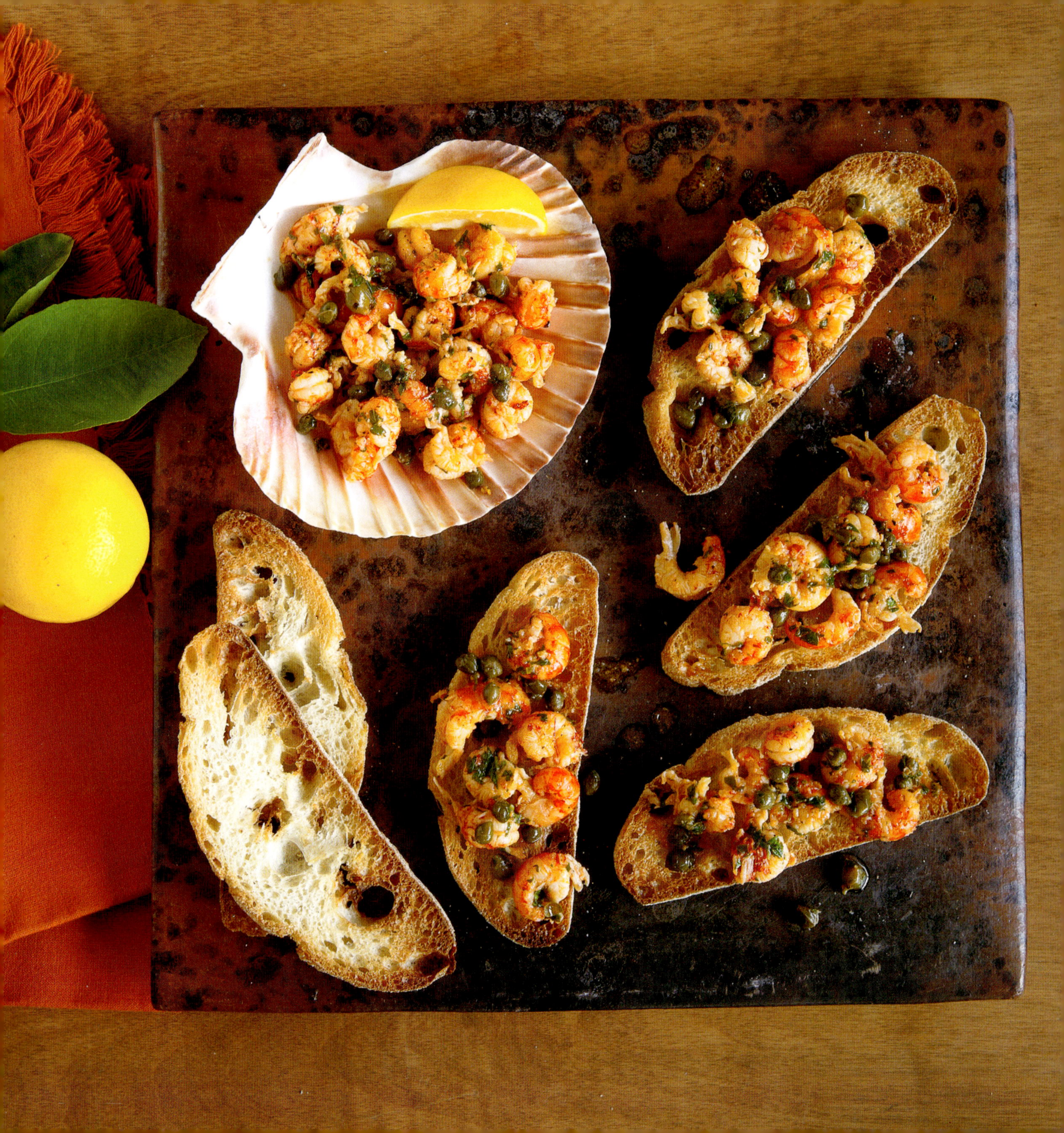

Crawfish with White Wine, Lemon & Capers

....

This tasty dish can be prepared before you've had time to finish your first glass of wine, which can be poured from the same bottle you're using in the recipe.

8	tablespoons butter
1	pound cooked crawfish tails
1	cup dry, white wine
1	tablespoon freshly squeezed lemon juice
1½	tablespoons capers, drained & rinsed
	Coarse salt & freshly ground black pepper
2	tablespoons chopped parsley
4	slices toasted bread

Melt butter in a large skillet on medium-high heat; when foaming subsides, add crawfish tails and cook, while stirring, for 2 minutes. Add wine, lemon juice and capers and cook, stirring occasionally, until sauce begins to thicken, about 4-5 minutes. Season to taste with salt and pepper. Add parsley. Serve over toasted bread.

Makes 4 servings.

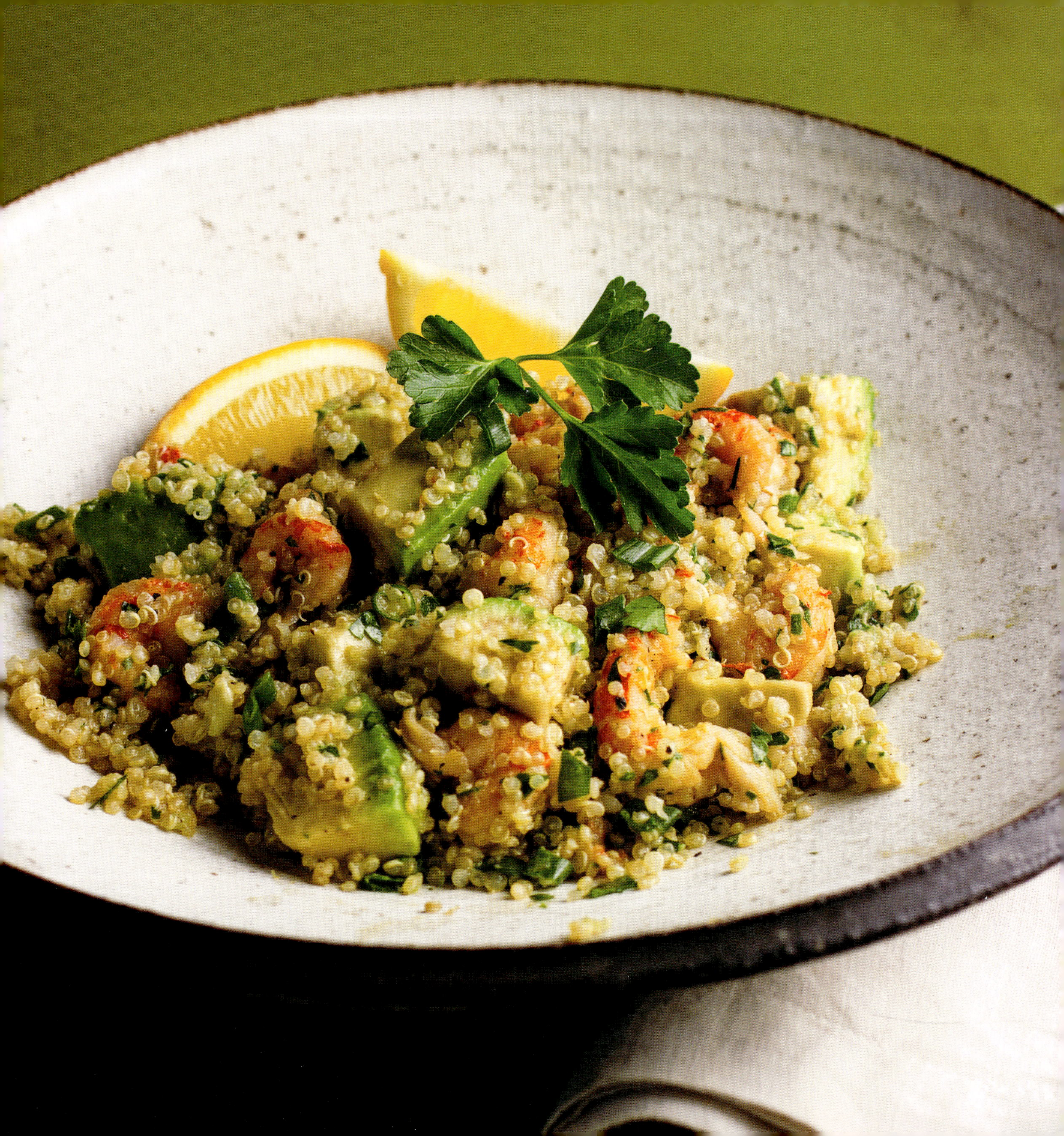

Salads & Appetizers

Crawfish, Avocado & Quinoa Salad

....

Quinoa (pronounced keen-wa) has acquired a trendy reputation in recent years, but don't let that put you off. In addition to being nutritious, this nutty-tasting grain (actually a seed) native to South America is also quite delicious and adaptable.

- 2 cups chicken stock or broth
- 1 cup quinoa
- ¼ cup extra-virgin olive oil
- 1 pound cooked crawfish tails
- ½ cup chopped green onion tops
- ½ cup chopped parsley
- Coarse salt & freshly ground black pepper
- Hot sauce
- 2 avocados
- 2 tablespoons freshly squeezed lemon juice

In a medium pot, bring stock or broth to a boil, add quinoa, stir, cover pot and simmer until all the stock is absorbed about 15 minutes. Remove from heat and leave undisturbed for 15 minutes. Turn cooked quinoa into a mixing bowl and slowly add olive oil while fluffing with a fork. Add crawfish and toss. Add onion tops and parsley, toss and season to taste with salt, black pepper and hot sauce.

Peel, seed and slice avocados and cut into bite-sized pieces. Add to mixing bowl, drizzle with lemon juice and toss gently.

Makes about 4 servings.

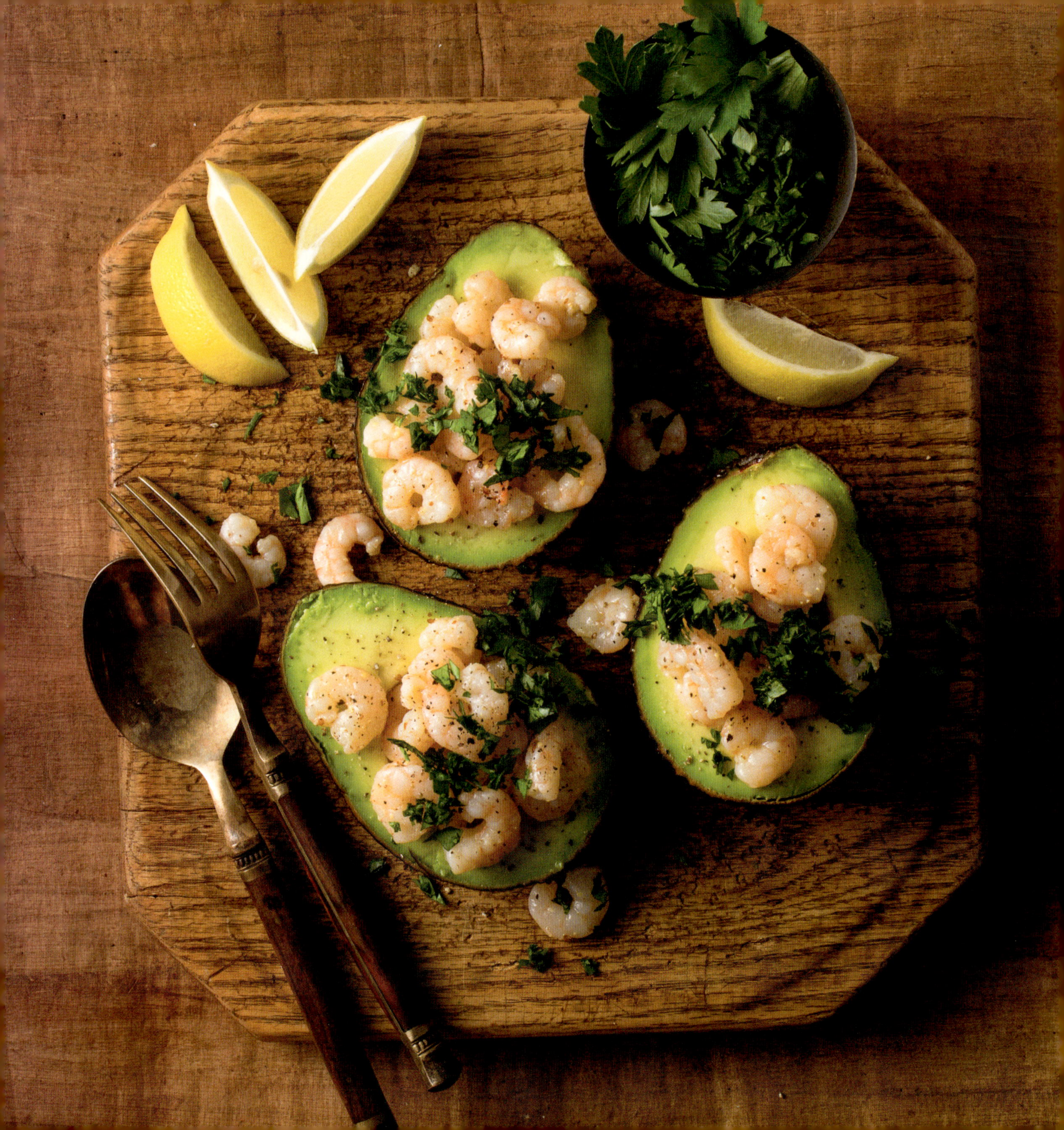

Avocados Stuffed with Shrimp

A quick and simple-to-prepare dish that only needs good bread, butter and a glass of wine.

2	avocados
1	pound cooked, small shrimp, chilled
¼	cup extra-virgin olive oil
4	teaspoons freshly squeezed lemon juice
1	teaspoon Creole mustard
	Coarse salt & freshly ground black pepper
	Hot sauce
1	teaspoon chopped parsley

Halve avocados and remove seeds Slice off a thin strip from the bottom of each half so avocado will sit flat on a plate. Place avocado halves on 4 plates. In a mixing bowl, make a vinaigrette with the oil and lemon juice. Add mustard and whisk to combine. Season with salt, pepper and hot sauce. Add shrimp and toss to combine. Adjust seasoning. Pile shrimp atop avocado halves and sprinkle with chopped parsley.

Makes 4 servings.

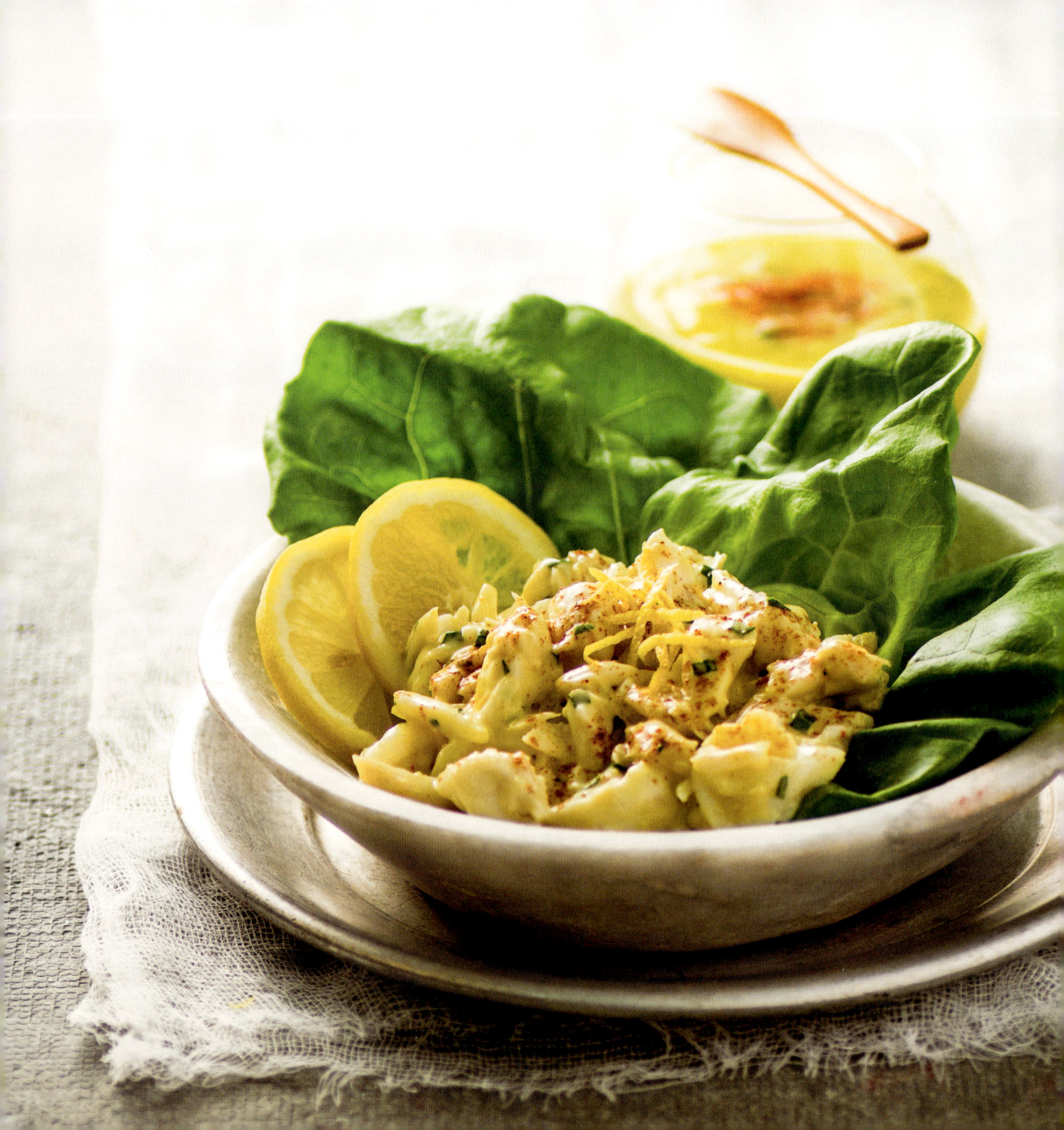

Crab Salad

....

The mayonnaise you make in the first step may seem strong and too thick, but when combined with the crabmeat the flavor and consistency are just right.

2	egg yolks
¼	teaspoon salt
1	teaspoon freshly squeezed lemon juice
½	cup extra-virgin olive oil
¼	cup vegetable oil
½	teaspoon grated lemon zest
1	teaspoon snipped chives
1	teaspoon chopped parsley
	Cayenne pepper
1	pound jumbo lump crabmeat, picked over
	Lettuce leaves
	Paprika for garnish

In a mixing bowl, beat egg yolks, salt and lemon juice with a wire whisk until pale yellow and creamy. Continue beating with whisk, while slowly adding oils, a drop at a time in the beginning. As the mixture emulsifies, increase slightly the amount of oil you are adding, while continuing to whisk, until all the oils have been added. Add lemon zest, chives and parsley; season to taste with cayenne and whisk to incorporate.

Add crabmeat and toss gently so as not to break up lumps. Cover and refrigerate until cold. To serve, line plates with lettuce leaves, spoon over crab salad and sprinkle with paprika.

Makes 4 servings.

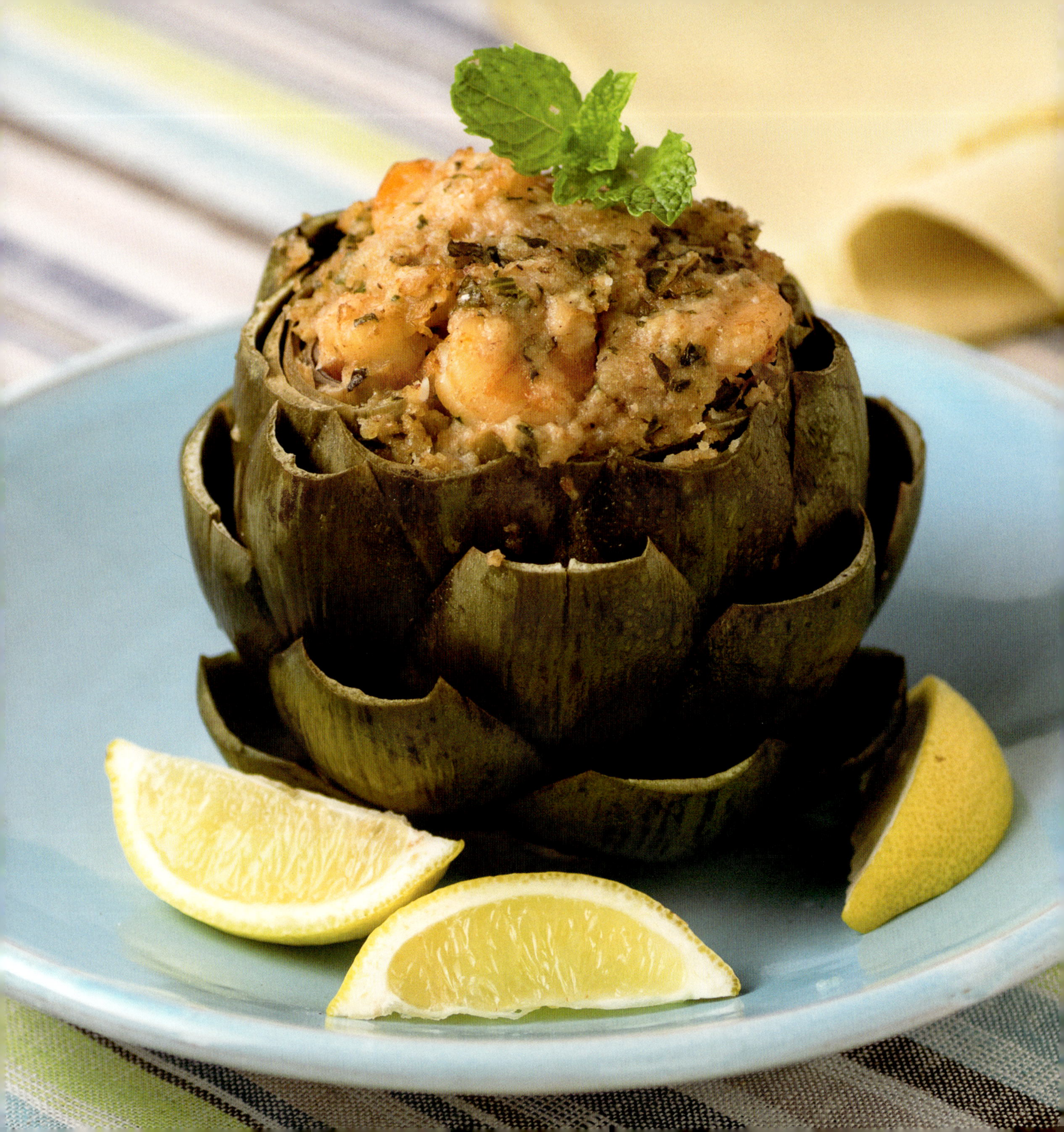

Salads & Appetizers

Artichokes Stuffed with Shrimp

....

Stuffed artichokes are a staple of New Orleans cuisine, one of many dishes with an Italian pedigree.

4   *artichokes*

1   *lemon*

1   *cup cooked & peeled small shrimp*

4   *cloves garlic, minced*

¼   *cup chopped parsley*

¼   *cup chopped mint*

1   *cup breadcrumbs*

½   *cup freshly grated Parmesan*

Coarse salt & freshly ground black pepper

Cayenne

2   *tablespoons freshly squeezed lemon juice*

1½   *cups extra-virgin olive oil, divided*

Lemon wedges

Fill a container large enough to hold the artichokes with water and squeeze in the juice of half a lemon. Cut off the stem of the artichoke and remove several layers of the large tough leaves. Rub all cut surfaces with half a lemon to prevent discoloration. Using a large knife, cut about 1 inch off the top of the artichoke, leaving a flat surface. Spread the artichoke open and, using a spoon, remove the choke. Place artichoke in the acidulated water and repeat with the others.

In a mixing bowl, combine shrimp, garlic, parsley, mint, breadcrumbs and Parmesan. Season to taste with salt, cayenne and black pepper. Add lemon juice and 1 cup of olive oil. Mix well and adjust seasoning. Invert and squeeze artichokes to remove water and place in a nonreactive pot large enough to hold them upright. Spread open the tops of artichokes and pack them with the shrimp mixture.

Pour water in the pot to come halfway up the artichokes. Add some salt and ½ cup olive oil. Place a square of wax paper on top of each artichoke and cover the pot. Bring to a boil, reduce heat and simmer until artichokes are tender, about 20 minutes. Remove artichokes and place in a serving dish. Serve hot, at room temperature or chilled, accompanied by lemon wedges.

Makes 4 servings.

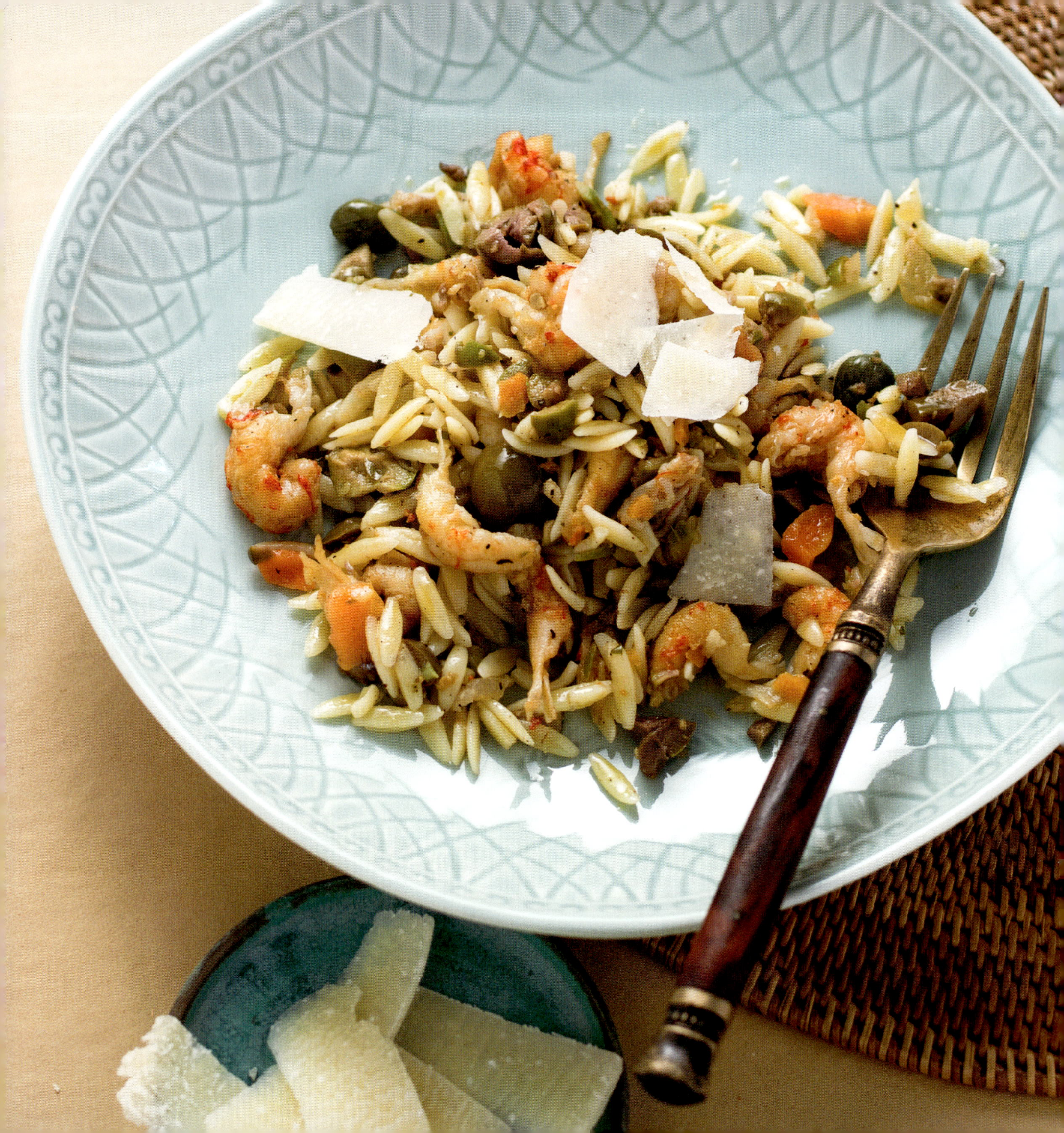

Crawfish with Olive Salad & Orzo

Olive salad is an essential ingredient in a muffuletta, but it also has other uses, as in this piquant dish with crawfish and orzo, a rice-shaped pasta. There are several good brands of olive salad on the market. The one I used for this recipe is Rouses.

1	pound orzo
3	tablespoons extra-virgin olive oil
2	cloves garlic, minced
1	pound cooked crawfish tails
1	cup olive salad
	Coarse salt & freshly ground black pepper
½	cup freshly grated Parmesan

Cook orzo according to package directions.

Meanwhile, in a large skillet over medium heat, cook garlic in oil until softened, about 2-3 minutes. Add crawfish tails and olive salad and cook, stirring frequently, until heated through, about 5 minutes.

Drain orzo and transfer to a large serving bowl. Add crawfish mixture and toss to combine. Season to taste with salt and pepper. Add Parmesan and toss.

Makes 6-8 servings.

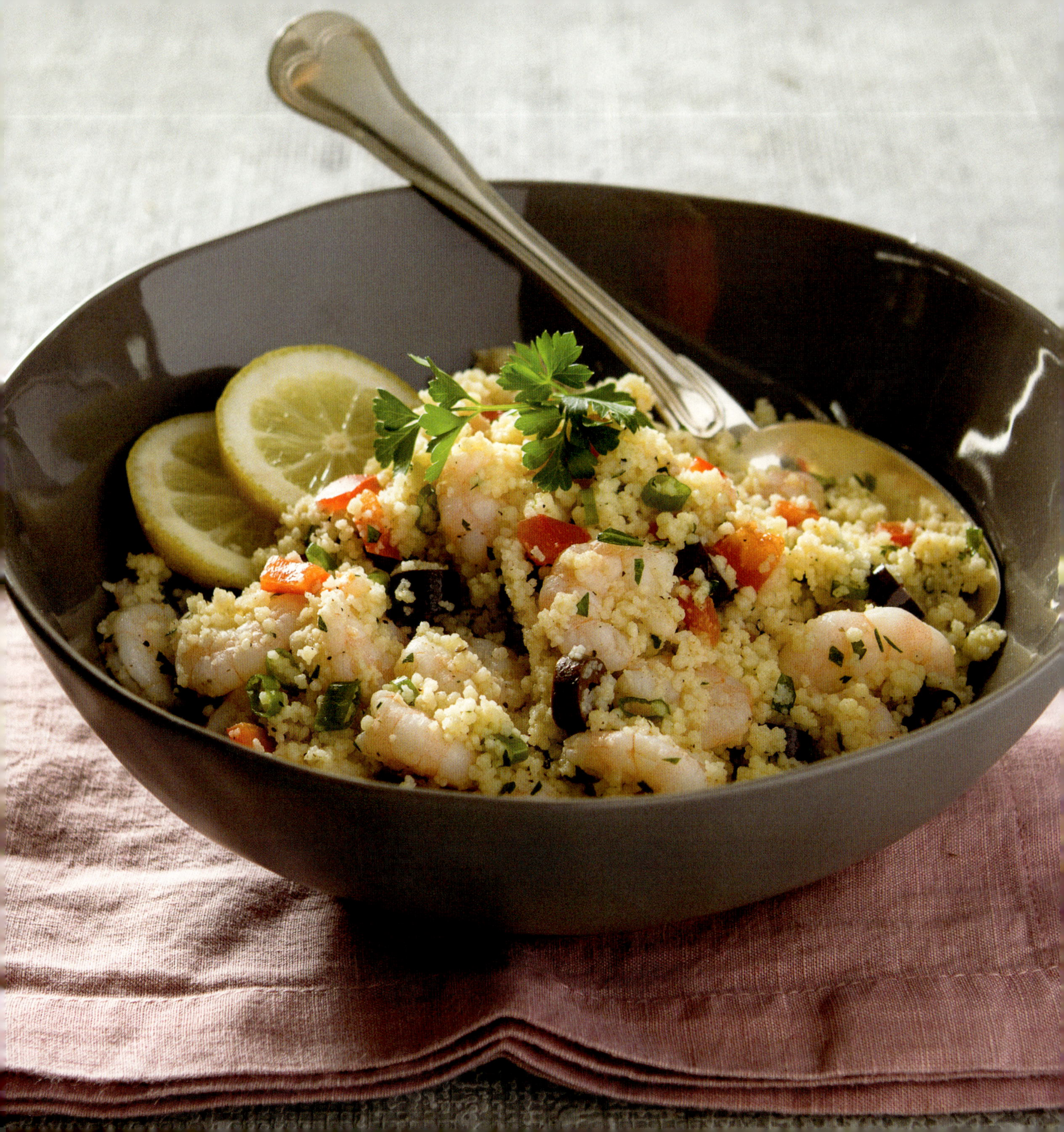

Shrimp & Couscous Salad

This is a far cry from the traditional way couscous is served in North Africa, but it's no less delicious for that.

- 1½ cups couscous
- ½ cup extra-virgin olive oil
- 1 pound cooked & peeled small shrimp
- 1 red bell pepper, seeded & diced
- ¾ cup small black olives
- 3 tablespoons chopped parsley
- 3 tablespoons chopped green onion tops
- 2 tablespoons freshly squeezed lemon juice
- Coarse salt & freshly ground black pepper
- Hot sauce

Cook couscous according to package instructions. Transfer cooked couscous to a mixing bowl and fluff with a fork while drizzling in olive oil. If there are lumps, separate grains with your fingers. Add shrimp, bell pepper and olives and toss to combine. Add parsley, onion tops and lemon juice, and toss to combine. Season to taste with salt, pepper and hot sauce. Serve chilled.

Makes 4 generous servings.

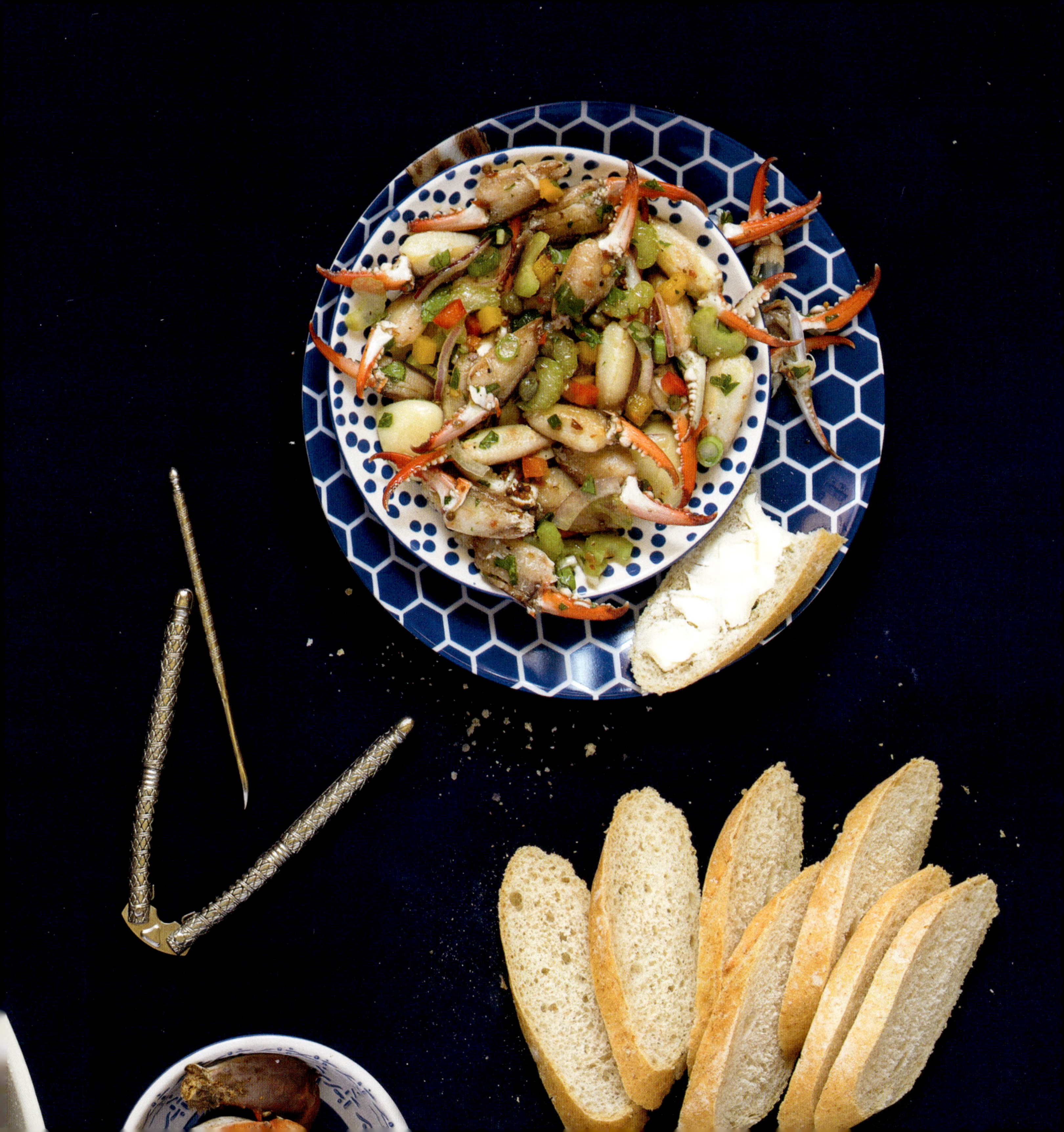

Marinated Crab Claws

Serve these with good crusty bread to dip in the marinade.

- 1 cup dry white wine
- 2 tablespoons crab boil (whole spices)
- 1 tablespoon crushed red pepper
- 1 teaspoon freshly ground black pepper
- 1 bay leaf
- 6 cloves garlic, peeled
- ½ cup chopped celery with leaves
- ½ cup chopped red onion
- ½ cup chopped red bell pepper
- ½ cup chopped yellow bell pepper
- ¼ cup chopped parsley
- ¼ cup chopped green onion tops
- 1 tablespoon capers, drained & rinsed
- ½ cup white wine vinegar
- ¼ cup freshly squeezed lemon juice
- 1 cup extra-virgin olive oil
- Hot sauce (optional)
- Cayenne pepper (optional)
- 1 pound cooked crab claws, cracked

In a nonreactive pan, combine white wine, crab boil, crushed red pepper, black pepper, bay leaf and garlic. Bring to a boil, reduce heat and simmer for 10 minutes. Cool. Combine cooled wine mixture with remainder of ingredients (except crab claws). Stir and adjust seasonings as desired. Place cracked crab claws in a flat, nonreactive container (an 8½ x 13-inch Pyrex dish is ideal) and pour marinade over. Cover with plastic wrap, refrigerate and marinate for 6 hours or longer, stirring occasionally.

Makes 4 servings as an appetizer.

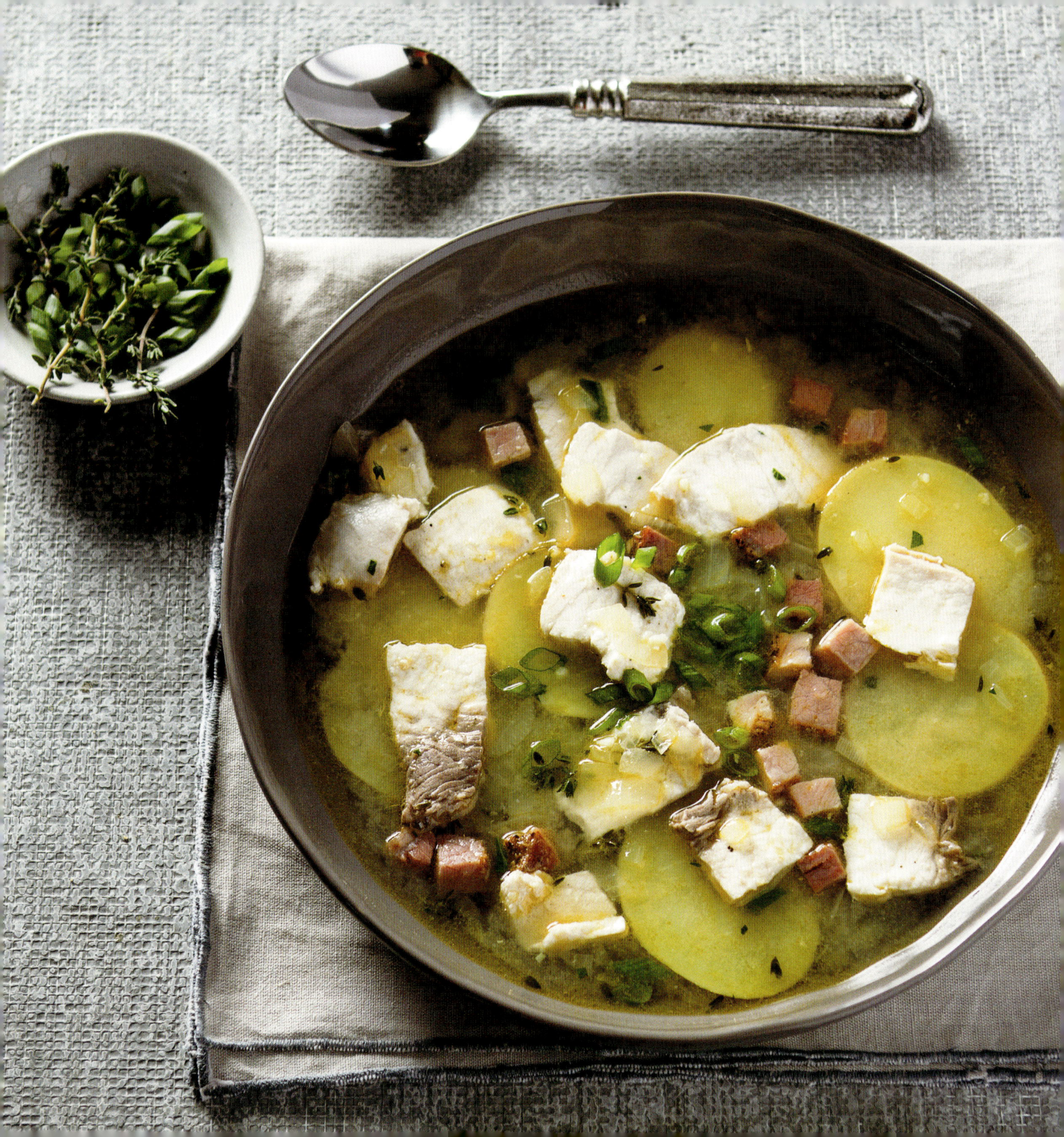

Gumbos & Soups

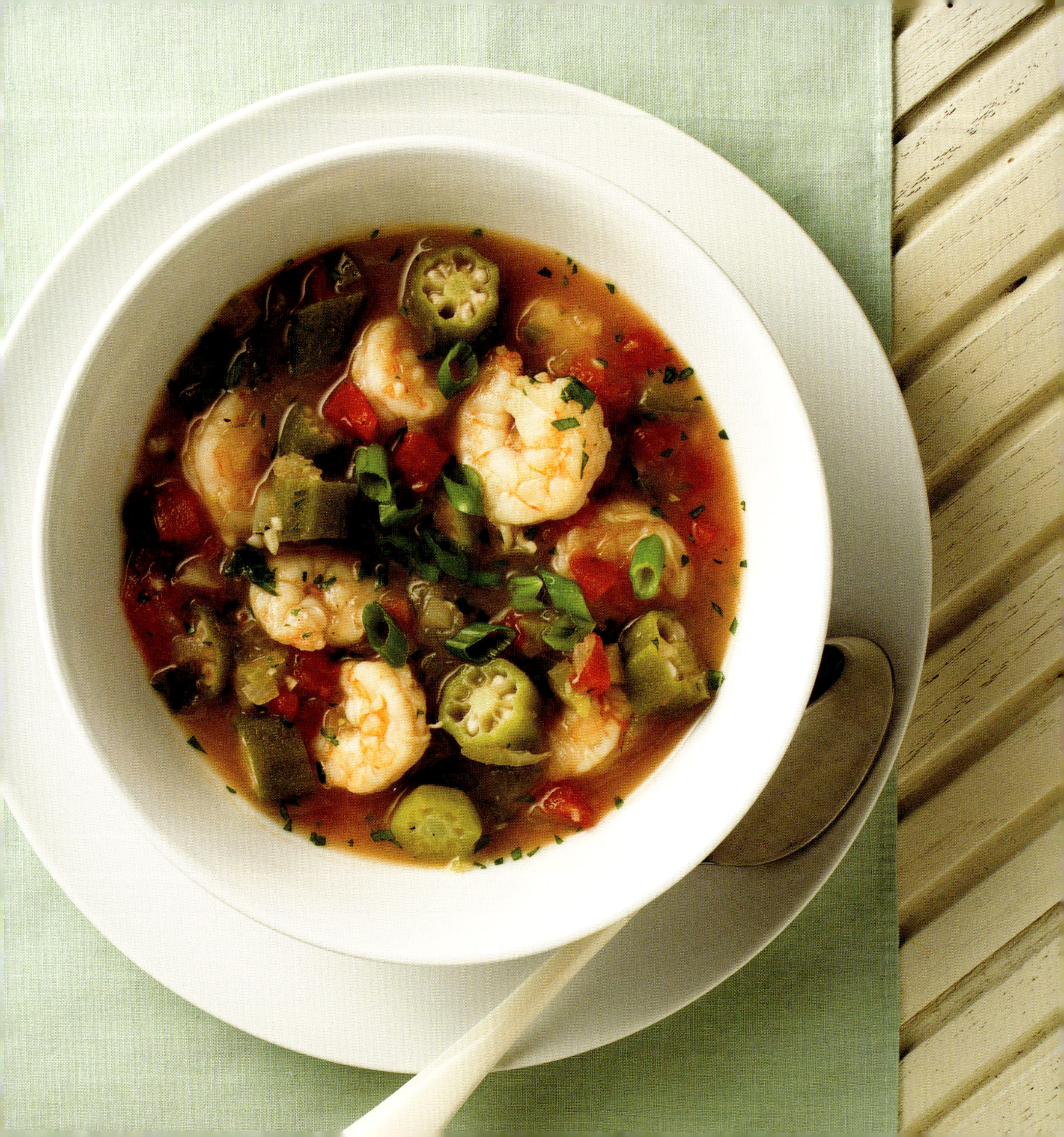

Shrimp & Okra Gumbo Light

The idea of a gumbo without roux is unthinkable to many, but there are ample precedents in early Louisiana cookbooks. This recipe has no added fat or flour, making it a good choice for dieters. Ground, dried shrimp is an excellent flavor-enhancer that can be used in a variety of preparations.

- 3 cups chicken stock or broth
- 1 (14.5 oz.) can petite diced tomatoes
- 1 large onion, chopped
- 1 large bell pepper, seeded & chopped
- 1 pound okra, trimmed & sliced
- 1 pound shrimp, peeled & deveined
- 4 teaspoons ground, dried shrimp
- Hot sauce
- Coarse salt & freshly ground black pepper
- ¼ cup chopped green onion tops
- ¼ cup chopped parsley

Combine broth, tomatoes, onion, bell pepper and okra in large pot. Bring to a boil, reduce heat and simmer, stirring occasionally, until okra is tender, about 60-90 minutes. Add shrimp, season to taste with ground, dried shrimp, hot sauce, salt and pepper, and simmer until shrimp turn pink, about 5 minutes. Add green onion tops and parsley.

Makes 4 servings.

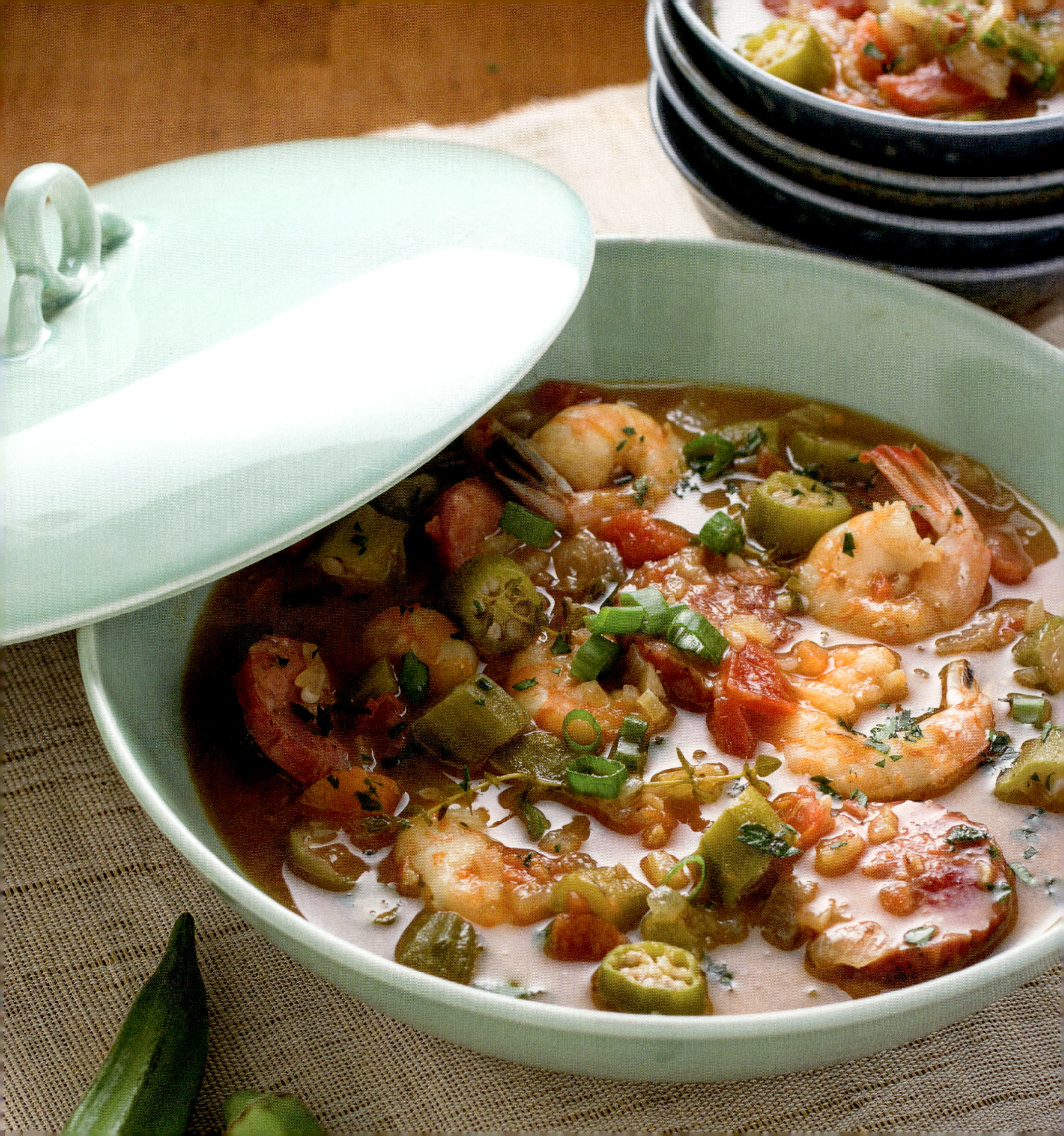

Shrimp, Andouille & Okra Gumbo

....

Shrimp are an ingredient in many different types of gumbo, limited only by the cook's imagination.

2	tablespoons extra-virgin olive oil
½	pound andouille, sliced
1	large onion, chopped
1	stalk celery, chopped
4	cloves garlic, minced
5	cups chicken stock or broth
1	tablespoon dark roux
1	(28-oz.) can diced tomatoes in juice
1	pound okra, trimmed & sliced
1	bay leaf
½	teaspoon whole thyme leaves
1	pound shrimp, peeled & deveined
	Coarse salt & freshly ground black pepper
	Hot sauce
¼	cup chopped parsley
¼	cup chopped green onion tops

In a large pot over medium heat, combine oil, andouille, onion, celery and garlic. Cook, stirring occasionally, until sausage begins to brown, about 15 minutes. Meanwhile, in a medium pot, bring chicken stock or broth to a boil. Add roux and whisk to dissolve.

When sausage has browned, add hot chicken broth, tomatoes with their juice, okra, bay leaf and thyme. Bring to a boil, reduce heat and simmer, stirring occasionally, until okra is tender, about 30 minutes. Add shrimp and cook until shrimp turn pink, about 5 minutes. Season to taste with salt, black pepper and hot sauce. Serve in large bowls with rice, garnished with chopped parsley and onion tops.

Makes 4-6 servings.

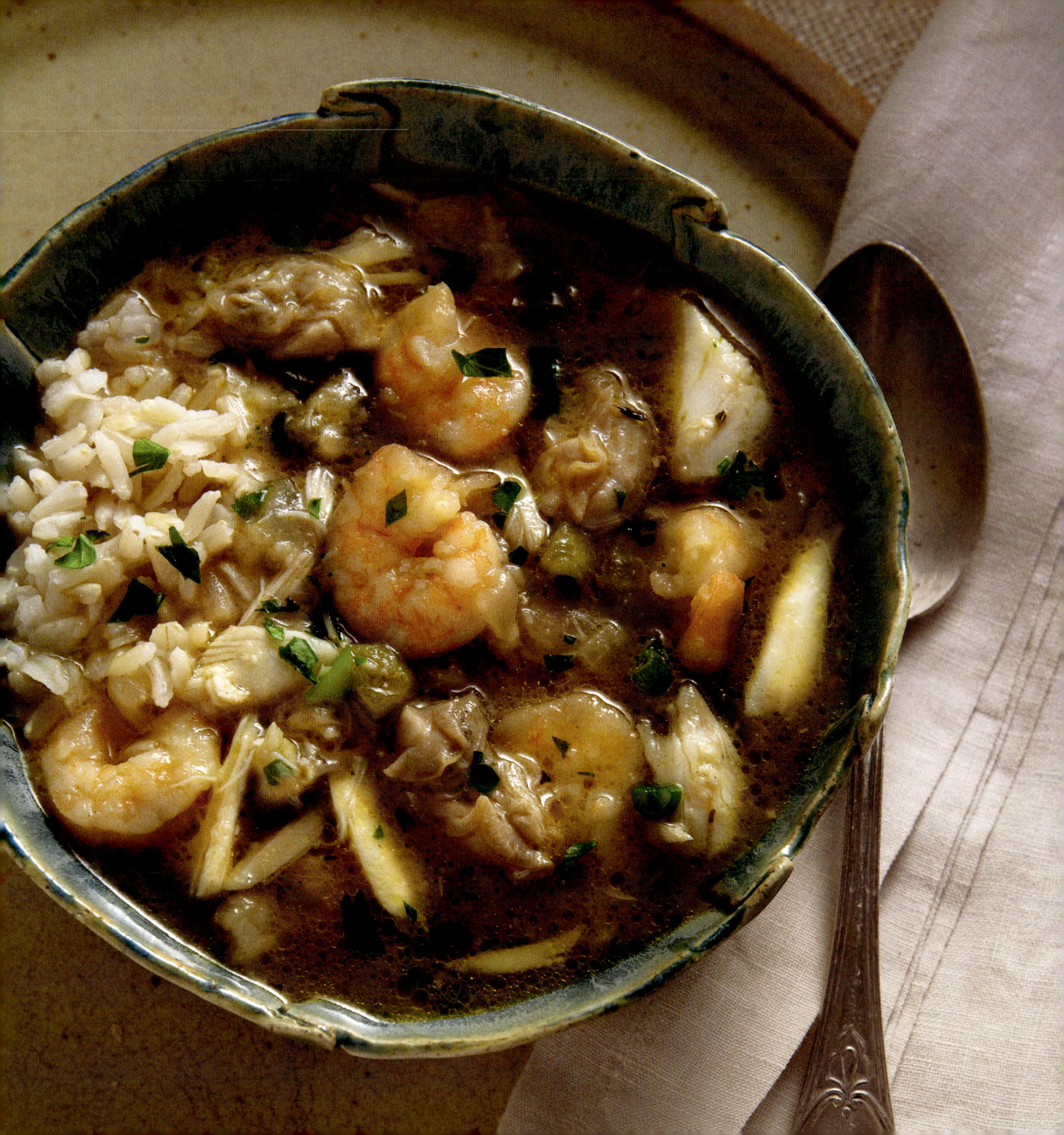

Shrimp, Oyster & Crabmeat Gumbo

This is an indulgent gumbo, made from three of the finest seafoods in the Gulf.

2	tablespoons olive or vegetable oil
1	large onion, diced
1	stalk celery, diced
2	cloves garlic, minced
¼	cup dark roux
8	cups chicken stock or broth
1	bay leaf
½	teaspoon dried thyme leaves
2	pounds medium shrimp, peeled & deveined
	Coarse salt & freshly ground black pepper
	Cayenne
	Hot sauce
1	pound lump crabmeat, picked over
1	pint shucked oysters
2	tablespoons chopped parsley
2	tablespoons chopped green onion tops

In a large pot, cook onion, celery and garlic in oil until softened, about 5 minutes. Add roux and stir to combine.

Slowly add chicken stock or broth to vegetable and roux mixture, while stirring, to combine. Add bay leaf and thyme, bring to a boil, reduce heat and simmer for about an hour.

Skim surface of gumbo. Add shrimp and cook for about 10 minutes. Season to taste with salt, peppers and hot sauce. Add crabmeat and oysters; cook until crabmeat is heated through and oysters begin to curl. Adjust seasonings. Add parsley and onion tops. Serve with steamed rice.

Makes about 4 servings.

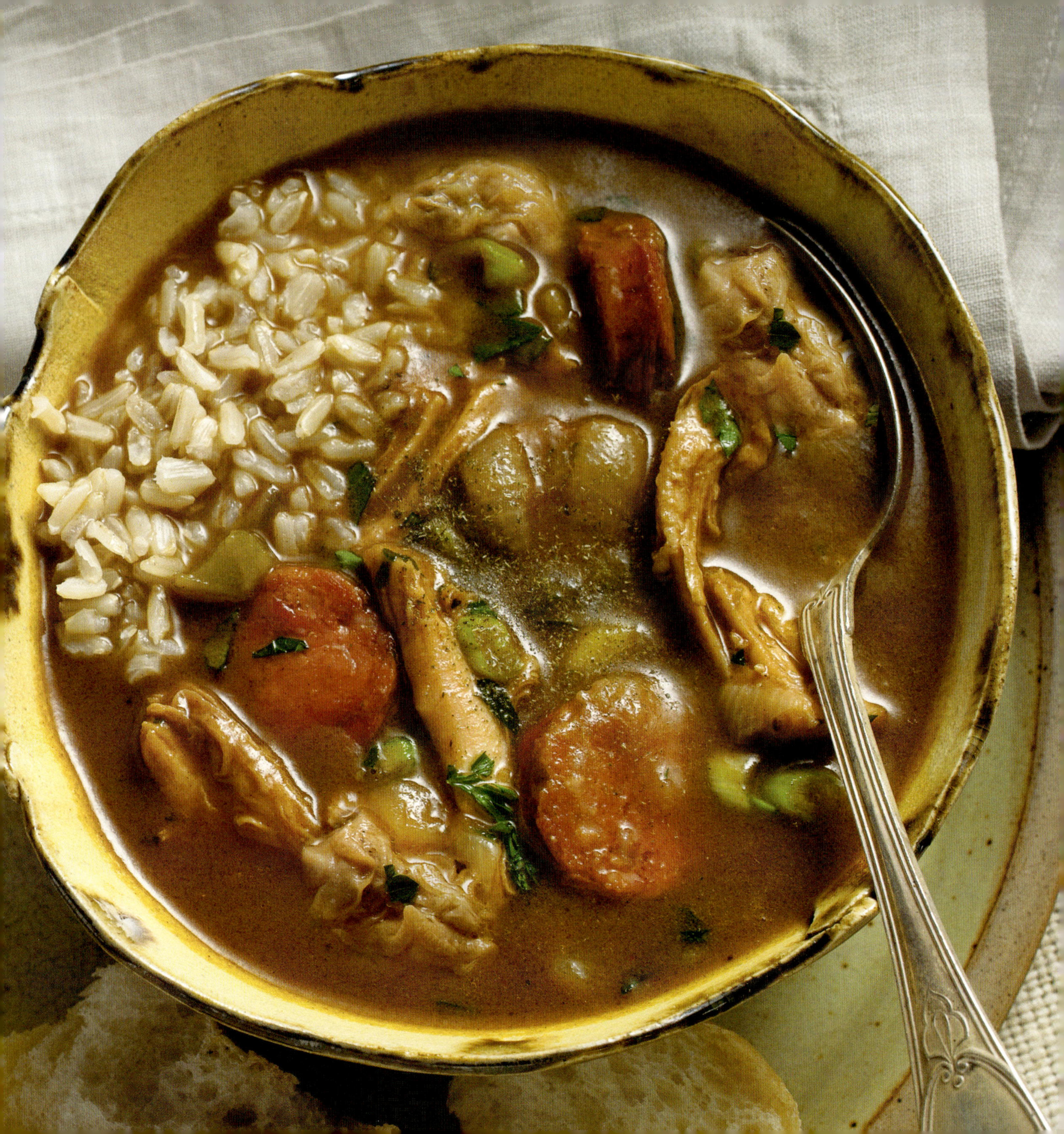

Duck, Andouille & Oyster Gumbo

This gumbo involves a number of steps and takes some time to prepare, but the result is fit for a holiday table.

1   domestic duck (5-6 pounds)
12 cups water
1   stalk celery, with leaves
6   cloves unpeeled garlic, smashed
2   bay leaves
1   teaspoon thyme leaves
1   ounce dried shiitake mushrooms
1   pound andouille, sliced
¼   cup all-purpose flour
2   medium onions, diced
1   bell pepper, diced
    Coarse salt & freshly ground black pepper
    Cayenne
2   dozen shucked oysters
¼   cup chopped parsley
¼   cup chopped green onion tops

Preheat oven to 400 degrees. Remove neck and giblets from duck cavity and rinse duck. With a sharp knife, remove wings and leg quarters; with kitchen shears, separate back from breast. Place duck pieces and giblets in roasting pan fitted with a rack, salt generously and roast in preheated oven until browned, about 1 hour.

Remove leg quarters and breast to a tray to cool. Transfer remaining pieces to a large pot. Strain rendered fat into a bowl and set aside. Scrape up any debris from roasting pan and add to pot. Add water, celery, garlic, bay leaves, thyme and shiitakes, bring to a boil, reduce heat, cover, and simmer. When legs and breast are cool enough to handle, remove skin and add to pot. Using a sharp knife, separate meat from bones and set aside. Add bones and any juices to pot, cover, and simmer for 1 hour or more.

Meanwhile, add sliced andouille to roasting pan and return to oven, stirring occasionally, until browned, about 30 minutes. Remove andouille and set aside. When duck broth is ready, strain into a heatproof container and keep warm. Reserve duck carcass.

In a heavy pot large enough to hold finished gumbo, heat ¼ cup of the rendered duck fat over medium heat, add flour and cook, stirring constantly, until dark brown. Turn off heat, add onions and stir. Add duck stock and bring to a boil while stirring. Add bell pepper. Cover and simmer for 30 minutes or more. Add andouille and simmer for an additional 30 minutes.

Cube reserved duck meat, pick meat from wings, back and neck and dice giblets. Add to gumbo. Season to taste with salt and peppers. Simmer for an additional 15 minutes and skim fat from surface. Add oysters and bring back to a simmer until oysters curl, about 5 minutes. Adjust seasonings, add chopped parsley and green onions. Serve with steamed rice.

Makes about 6 to 8 servings.

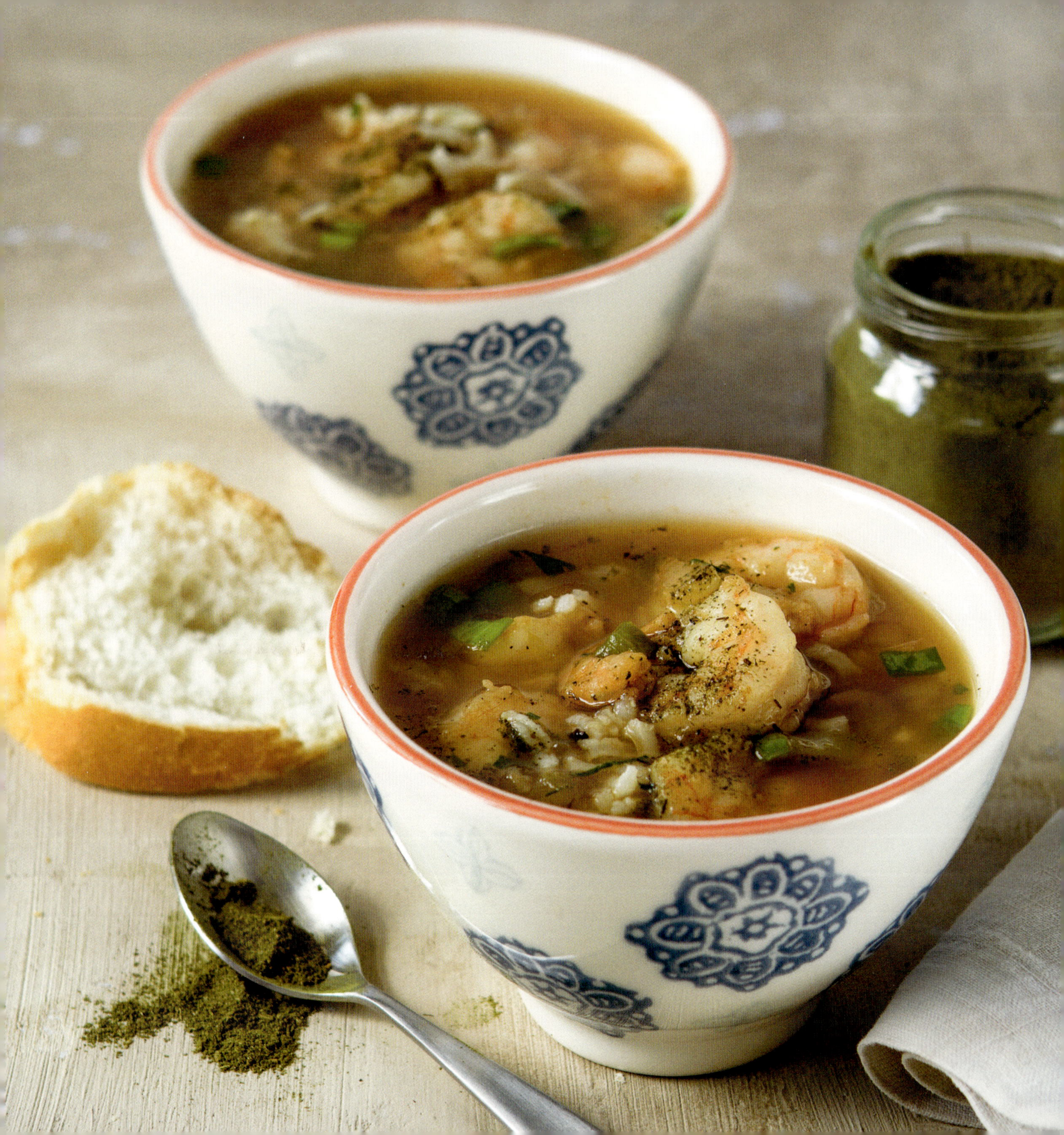

Shrimp Filé Gumbo

A homestyle gumbo—simple, quick and satisfying.

4	*pounds medium heads-on shrimp*
12	*cups water*
¼	*cup dry roux*
⅓	*cup dried shrimp*
1	*large onion, diced*
1	*bell pepper, diced*
4	*cloves garlic, minced*
½	*teaspoon dried thyme leaves*
1	*bay leaf*
	Cajun/Creole seasoning
	Coarse salt & freshly ground black pepper
	Hot sauce
¼	*cup chopped parsley*
¼	*cup chopped green onion tops*
	Filé

In a large pot, cover shrimp with water and bring to a boil. Place a colander over another large pot and drain shrimp, reserving the liquid they were cooked in. Place pot with liquid on stove. Whisk dry roux into pot until dissolved. Add dried shrimp, onion, bell pepper, garlic, thyme and bay leaf, and bring to a boil. Maintain the pot at a slow boil. Meanwhile, remove heads from shrimp, peel and devein them, and cook the rice. Add shrimp to gumbo, season to taste with Cajun/Creole seasoning, salt, pepper and hot sauce. Simmer for about 15 minutes. Add parsley and onion tops. Serve gumbo with filé and rice.

Makes 4 or more servings.

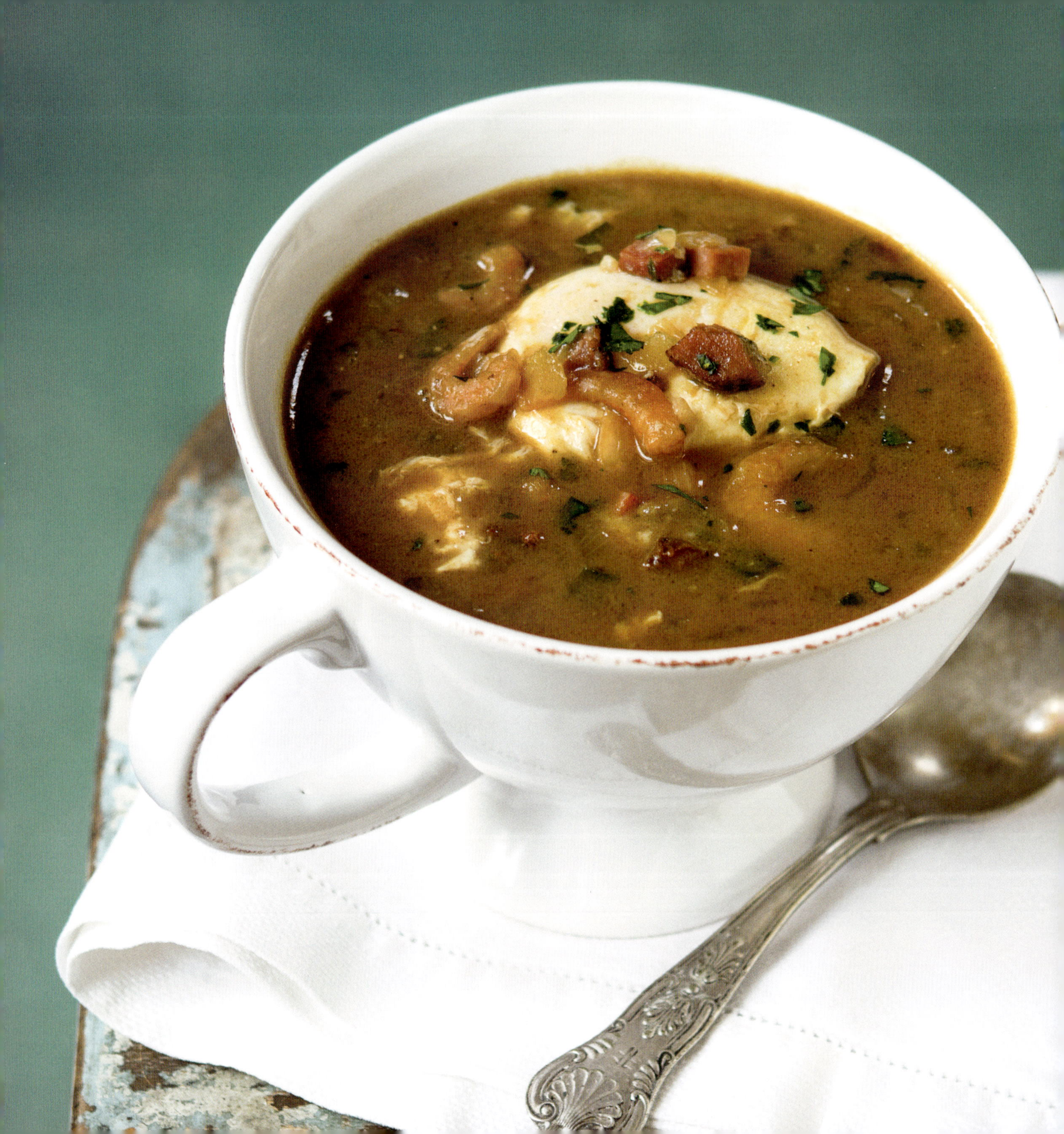

Dried Shrimp & Tasso Gumbo with Poached Eggs

....

Dried shrimp give this gumbo an intense flavor. Bottled roux and canned chicken broth cut preparation time to a minimum. Because the dried shrimp are salty, additional salt is usually not necessary. The gumbo can be served over rice in the conventional manner, but this is one version I prefer without rice.

1	tablespoon vegetable or olive oil
2	cloves garlic, minced
1	onion, diced
1	stalk celery, diced
3	cups low-sodium chicken broth
3	cups water
2	tablespoons dark roux
½	cup dried shrimp
½	cup diced tasso
	Freshly ground black pepper
	Hot sauce
4	eggs
1	tablespoon fresh parsley, chopped
2	tablespoons green onion tops, chopped
	Filé

In a large pot, heat oil and cook garlic, onions and celery until softened, about 5 minutes. Add chicken broth and water and bring to a boil. Add roux and whisk to dissolve. Add shrimp and tasso. Reduce heat to low and simmer for 30 minutes. Skim surface to remove excess oil. Season to taste with pepper and hot sauce.

Bring gumbo to a slow boil. Break eggs into gumbo and poach until whites are cooked, but yolks are still runny, about 3 minutes.

Ladle the gumbo into bowls, topping each serving with a poached egg. Garnish with parsley and onion tops. Serve with filé and rice, if desired.

Makes 4 servings.

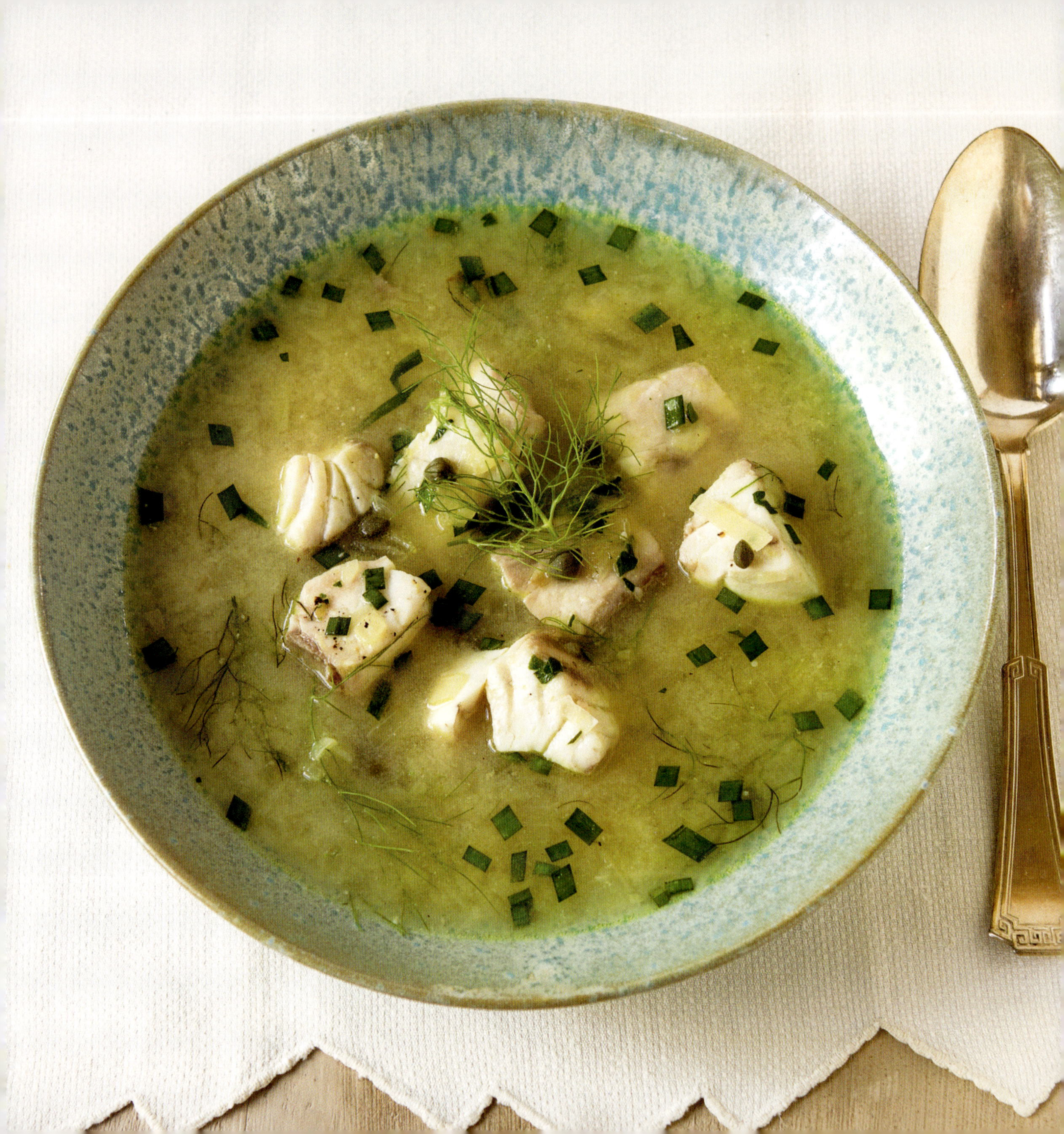

Green Redfish Soup

The clam juice in this recipe is salty, so taste before adding additional salt.

2	tablespoons extra-virgin olive oil
1	medium onion, chopped
¼	cup minced shallots
3	cups chicken stock or broth
1	cup bottled clam juice
½	cup dry white wine
1	pound redfish cut into small chunks
2	tablespoons lime juice
4	teaspoons capers, drained & rinsed
	Coarse salt & freshly ground black pepper
¼	cup chopped fresh dill
2	tablespoons chopped parsley
2	tablespoons minced chives

In a medium pot, combine olive oil, onion and shallots, cover and cook over medium heat until softened, about 5 minutes. Add chicken stock or broth, clam juice and white wine; bring to a boil, cover, reduce heat and simmer for 10 minutes. Uncover, add fish, return to a boil, then simmer until cooked through, about 5 minutes. Add lime juice and capers, season to taste with salt (if needed) and pepper. Add dill, chives and parsley.

Makes 4 servings.

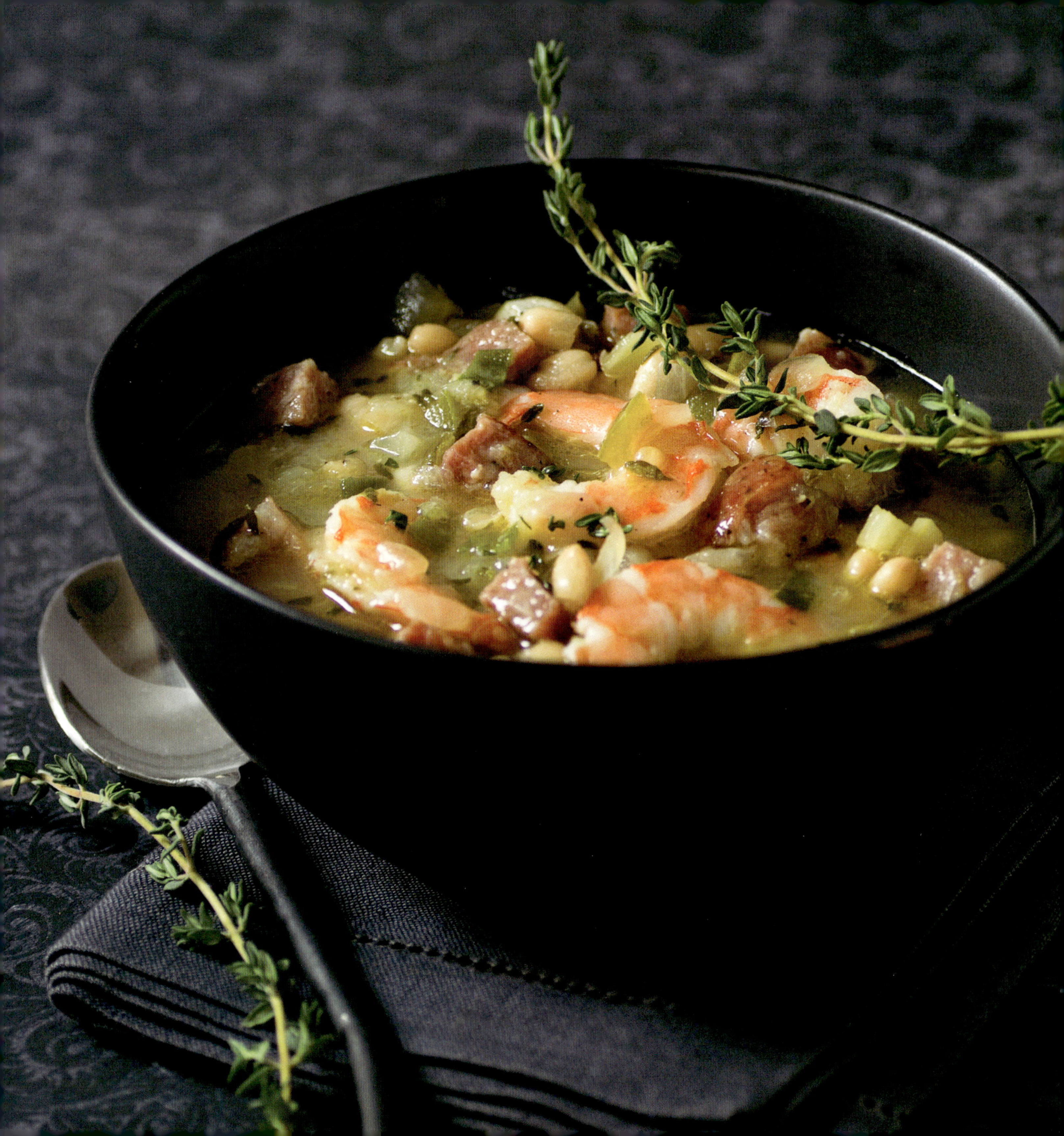

Navy Bean, Andouille & Shrimp Soup

Red beans are inextricably associated with Louisiana cooking, but white beans are also a staple in some areas.

1	cup navy beans
2	tablespoons extra-virgin olive oil
1	medium onion, chopped
2	cloves garlic, minced
1	bell pepper, chopped
1	rib celery, chopped
⅓	pound andouille, diced
4	cups chicken stock or broth
1	bay leaf
⅛	teaspoon thyme leaves
1	pound shrimp, peeled & deveined
	Coarse salt & freshly ground black pepper
¼	cup chopped parsley
¼	cup chopped green onion tops

Cover beans with water and soak overnight. Drain.

In a medium pot over medium heat, combine oil, onion, garlic, pepper, celery and andouille; cover and cook until softened, about 5 minutes. Add beans, chicken stock or broth, bay leaf and thyme. Bring to a boil, reduce heat, cover and simmer until beans are softened, about 40 minutes. Using the back of a large spoon, mash some of the beans against the side of the pot to thicken soup. Cook until soup is creamy, about 10 minutes. Add shrimp and cook 5 minutes. Season to taste with salt and pepper, add parsley and onion tops. If soup is too thick, thin with additional broth or water.

Makes 4-6 servings.

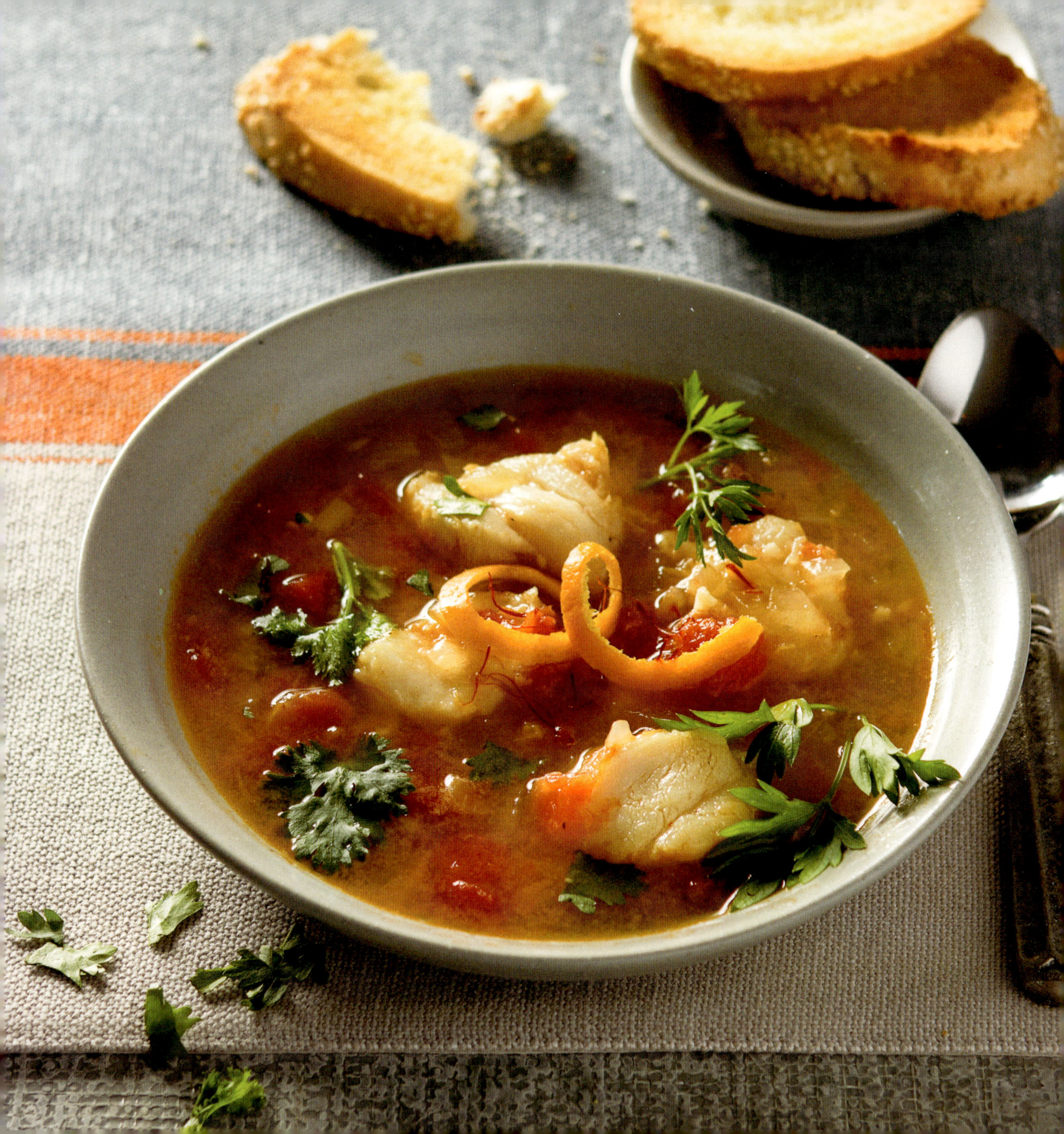

Saffron Seafood Soup

The dried shrimp in this recipe are salty, so additional salt is not required.

½	cup extra-virgin olive oil
2	medium onions, chopped
8	cloves garlic, minced
½	cup dried shrimp
2	cups diced tomatoes in juice
5	cups chicken stock or broth
½	cup dry white wine
¼	teaspoon saffron, crumbled
1	bay leaf
1	large strip orange peel
1	pound firm white fish, cut into small chunks
	Freshly ground black pepper
	Cayenne pepper
6	tablespoons chopped parsley
6	tablespoons chopped cilantro

In a medium pot, combine oil, onion and garlic; cover and cook over medium heat until softened, about 5 minutes. Meanwhile, in a food processor, grind dried shrimp to a coarse powder. Add ground shrimp, tomatoes and juice, chicken stock or broth, wine, saffron, bay leaf and orange peel to the pot. Bring to a boil, reduce heat, cover and simmer for 10 minutes. Uncover, add fish, bring back to a boil, then reduce heat and simmer until fish is cooked through, about 5 minutes. Season to taste with peppers, then add parsley and cilantro.

Makes 4 servings.

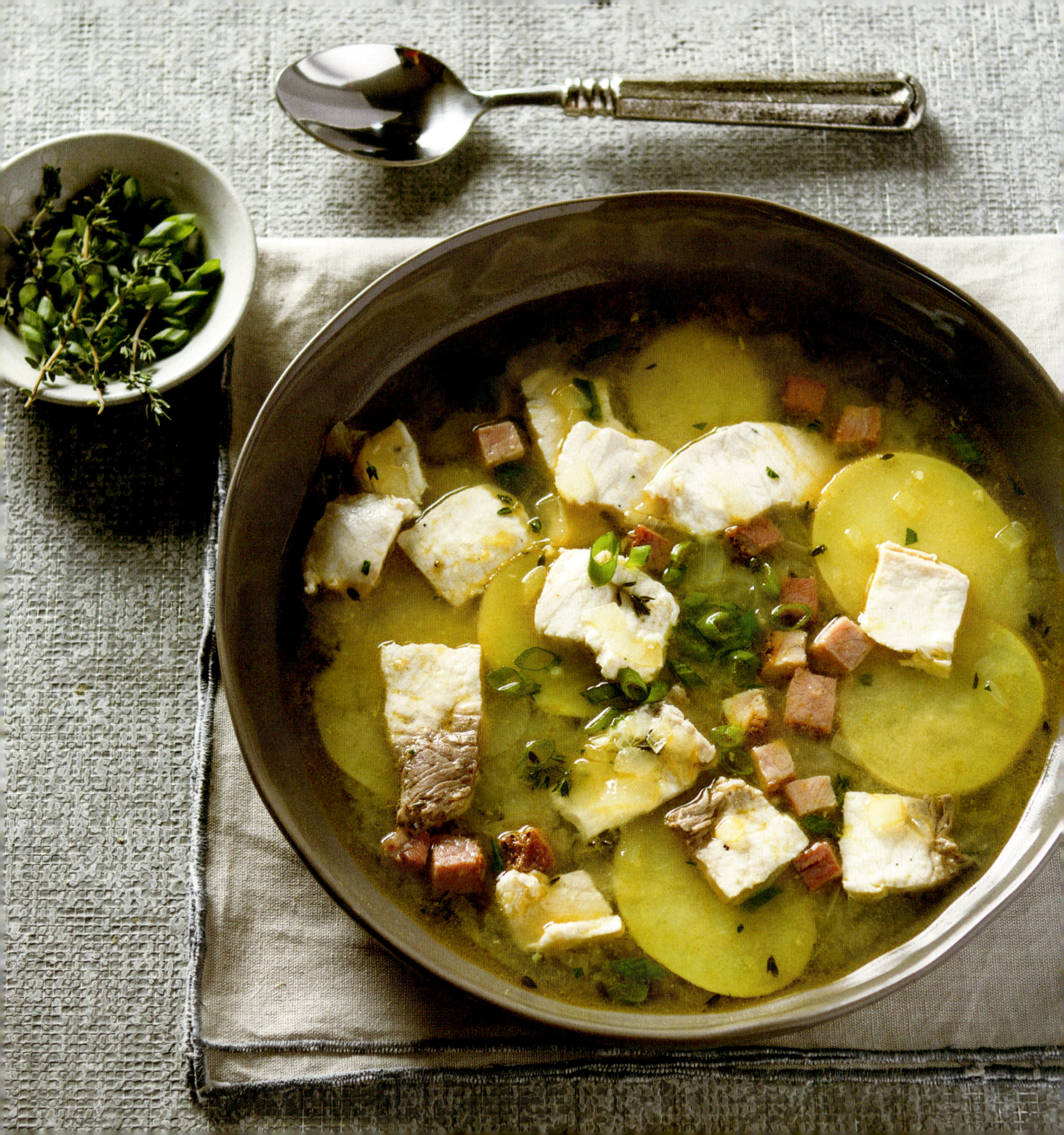

Swordfish, Tasso & Potato Soup

If swordfish is not available, other firm-fleshed fish can be substituted.

- ¼ cup extra-virgin olive oil
- 1 medium onion, chopped
- 2 cloves garlic, minced
- 1 cup diced tasso
- 2 medium potatoes, peeled & thinly sliced
- 4 cups chicken stock or broth
- ½ cup dry white wine
- 1 bay leaf
- ¼ teaspoon dried thyme leaves
- 8 ounces swordfish, thinly sliced
- Coarse salt & freshly ground black pepper
- 3 tablespoons freshly squeezed lemon juice
- ¼ cup chopped parsley
- ¼ cup chopped green onion tops

In a medium pot over medium heat, combine oil, onion, garlic and tasso; cover and cook until softened, about 5 minutes. Add potatoes, chicken stock or broth, wine, bay leaf and thyme; bring to a boil, reduce heat, cover and simmer until potatoes are softened, about 20 minutes. Add swordfish, bring to a boil, reduce heat and simmer until fish is cooked through, about 5 minutes. Season to taste with salt and pepper. Add parsley and green onion tops.

Makes 4 servings.

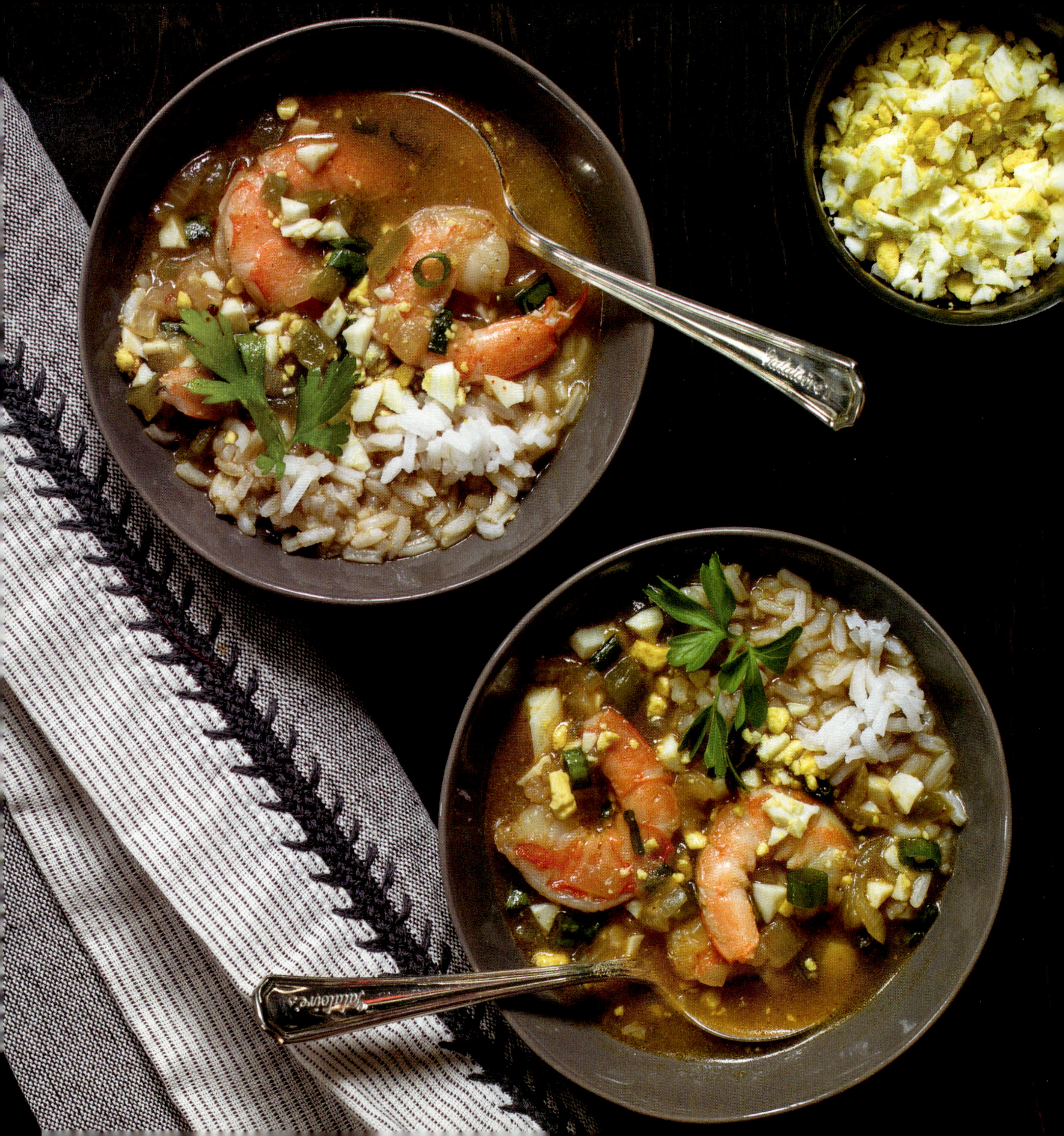

Etouffées & Stews

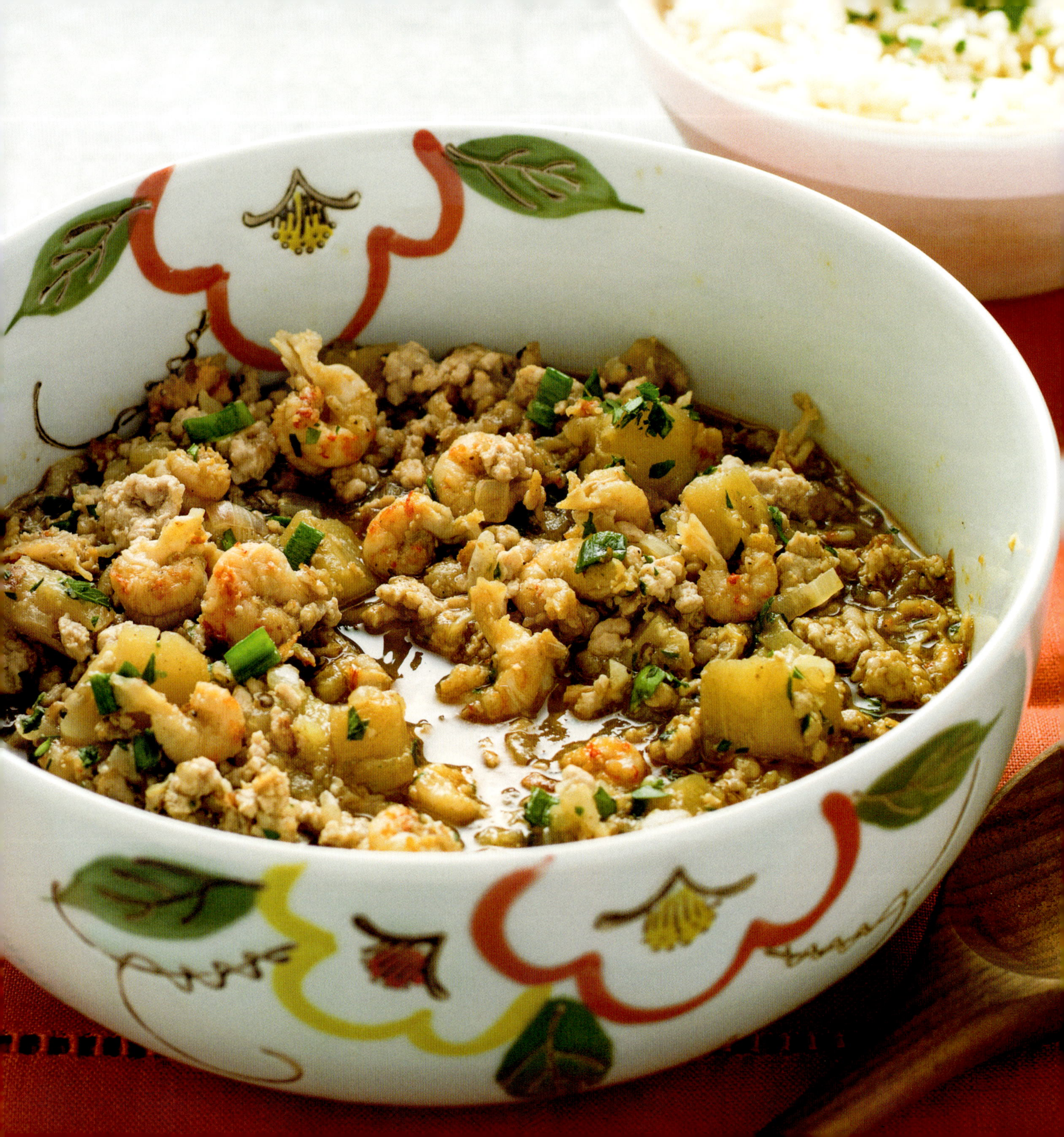

Crawfish & Eggplant Stew

Crawfish combine well with a variety of ingredients, including pork and eggplant, as in this recipe.

- 2 tablespoons olive oil
- 1 medium onion, chopped
- 4 cloves garlic, minced
- ½ pound ground pork
- ½ pound eggplant, cubed
- 3 cups chicken stock or broth
- 1 pound crawfish tails
- 1 tablespoon Cajun/Creole seasoning
- ¼ cup chopped parsley
- ¼ cup chopped green onion tops

In a heavy pot, cook onion and garlic in olive oil on high heat, stirring frequently, until onion begins to brown. Add pork and cook, stirring, until it browns. Add eggplant and chicken broth, bring to a boil, reduce heat and simmer, covered, stirring occasionally, until tender, about 5 minutes. Add crawfish and Cajun/Creole seasoning and simmer for 15 minutes. Adjust seasoning, add parsley and green onion tops. Serve over steamed rice.

Makes 4-6 Servings.

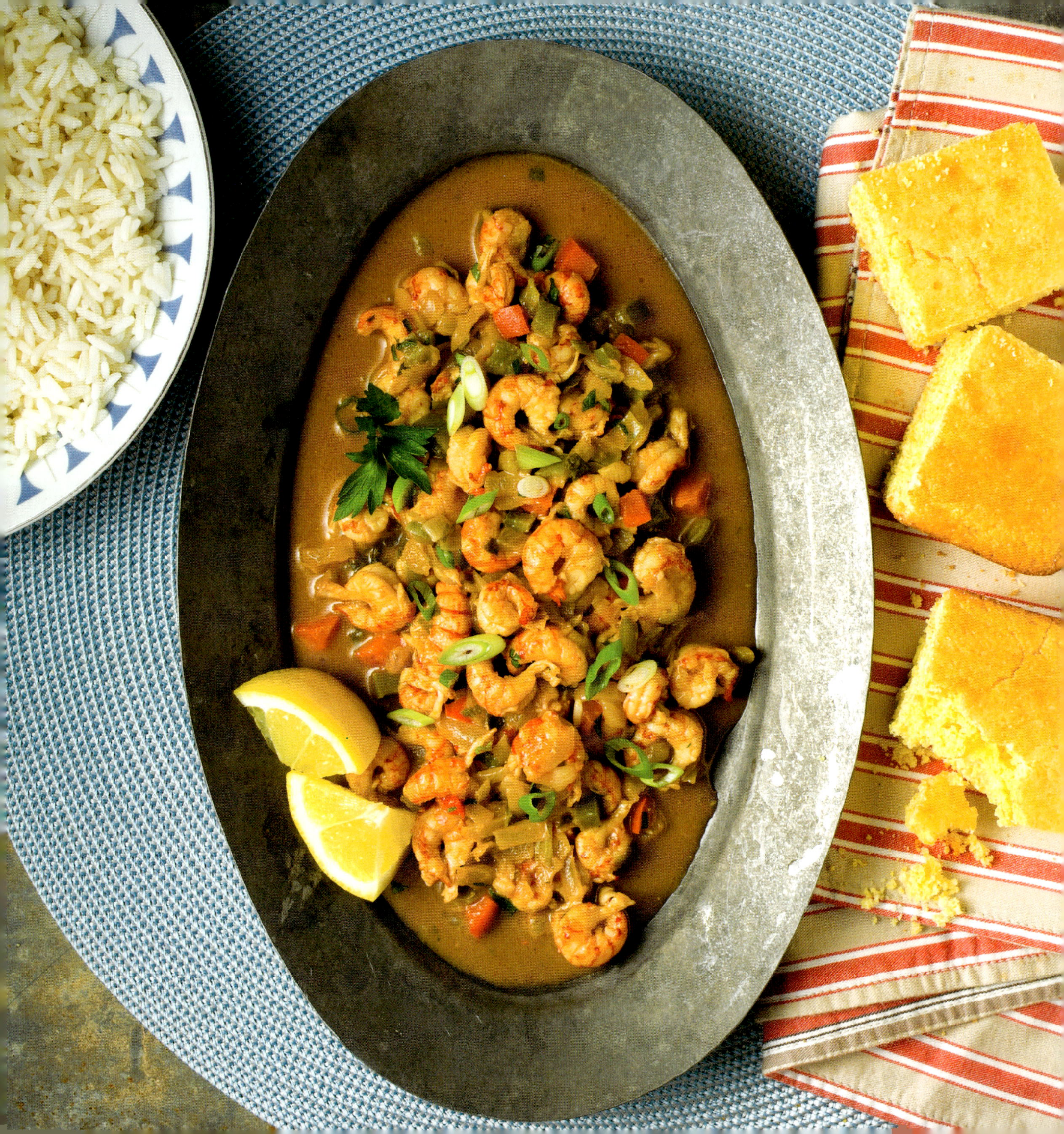

Quick Crawfish Stew

A quick and easy preparation suitable for a weeknight dinner.

2	cups chicken stock or broth
3	tablespoons dry roux
4	tablespoons butter
2	cups frozen seasoning vegetables
1	pound crawfish tails
2	tablespoons lemon juice
	Coarse salt & freshly ground black pepper
	Cayenne pepper

In a heavy pot over high heat, whisk roux into chicken stock or broth until dissolved. Add butter, vegetables and crawfish; bring to a boil, reduce heat and simmer until thickened and crawfish are tender, about 30 minutes. Add lemon juice and season to taste with salt and peppers. Serve over steamed rice.

Makes 4 servings.

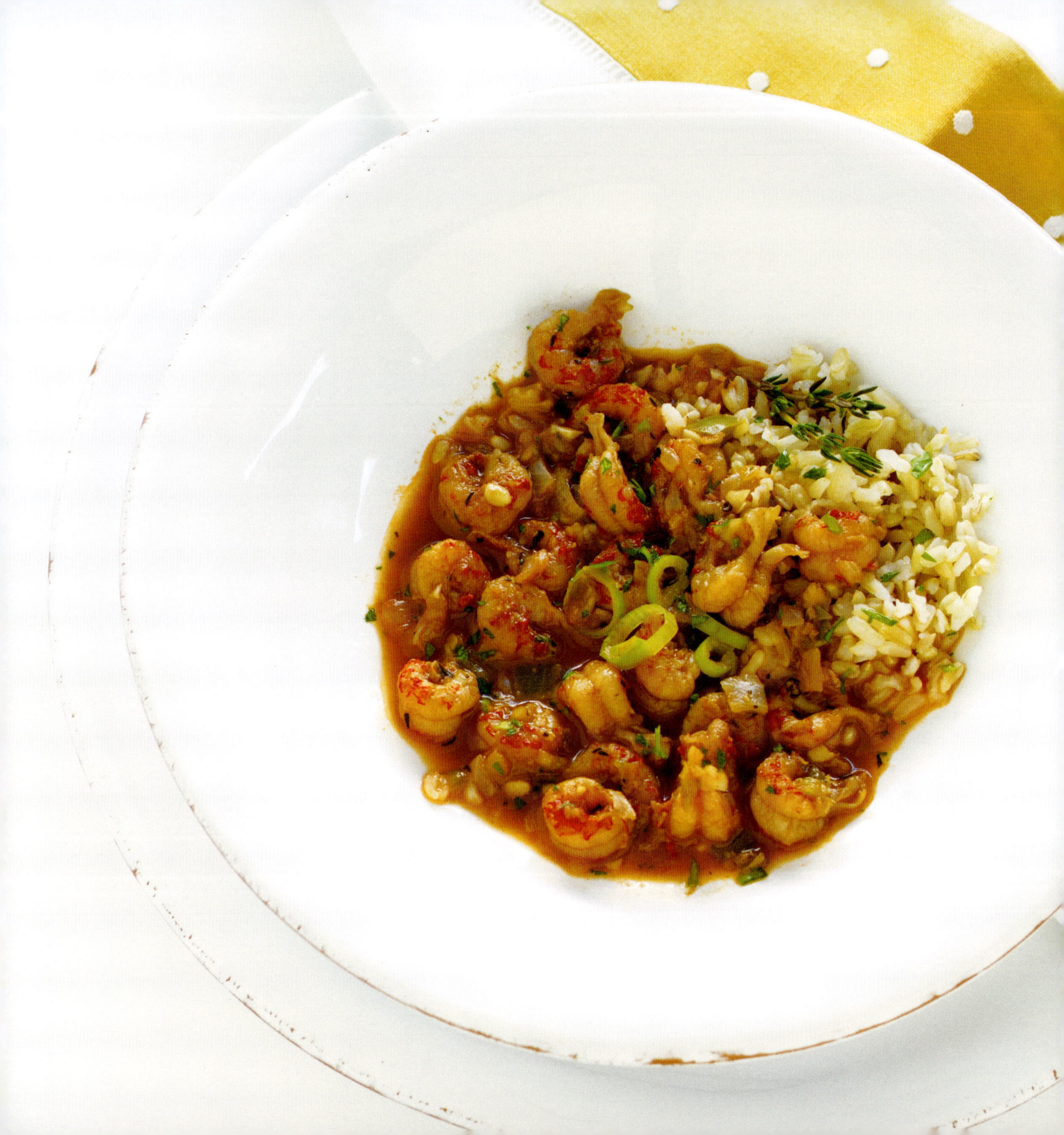

Crawfish Stew Light

This recipe can be prepared in short order.

2	cups chicken stock or broth
3	tablespoons dry roux
2	cloves garlic, minced
1	medium onion, chopped
1	stalk celery, chopped
1	bell pepper, chopped
1	bay leaf
½	teaspoon dried thyme leaves
1	pound crawfish tails, with fat
2	tablespoons lemon juice
	Cajun/Creole seasoning
	Coarse salt & freshly ground black pepper
	Hot sauce
2	tablespoons chopped parsley
2	tablespoons chopped green onion tops

In a heavy pot over high heat, whisk roux into chicken stock or broth until dissolved. Add garlic, onion, celery, bell pepper, bay leaf and thyme. Bring to a boil, reduce heat and simmer, stirring occasionally, for 30 minutes. Add crawfish tails and lemon juice; season to taste with Cajun/Creole seasoning, salt, pepper and hot sauce. Simmer, stirring occasionally, for 15 minutes. Add parsley and green onion tops. Serve over steamed rice.

Makes 4 servings.

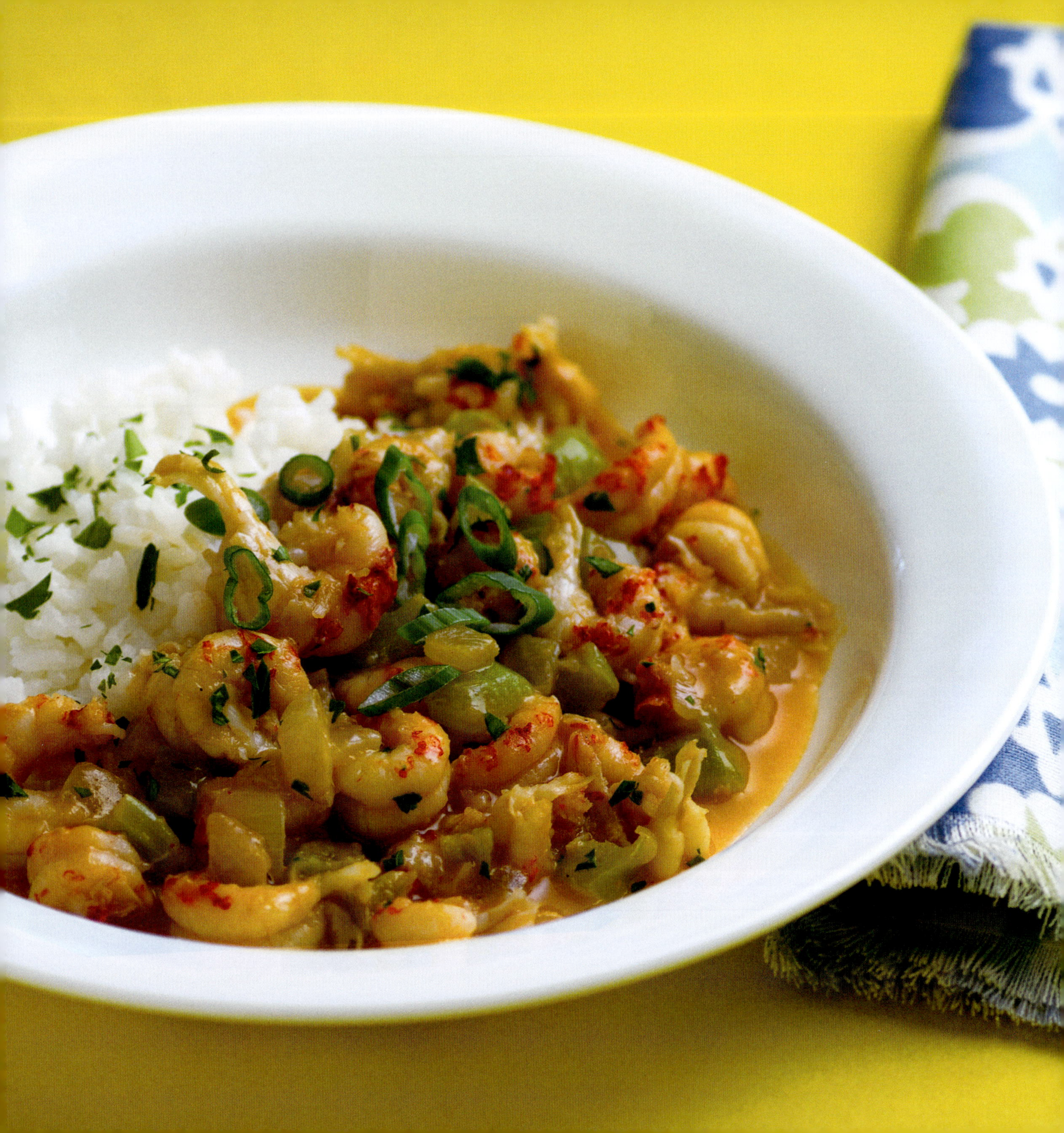

30-Minute Crawfish Etouffée

This doesn't take much longer to prepare than the rice you serve it with, and it's just about as easy.

- 2 *cups chicken stock or broth*
- ¼ *cup all-purpose flour*
- ½ *cup butter*
- 2 *cups frozen seasoning vegetables*
- 1 *pound crawfish tails*
- *Coarse salt & cayenne*

In a heavy pot, combine chicken stock or broth and flour; whisk until smooth. Add butter, vegetables and crawfish and bring to a boil. Reduce heat, season to taste with salt and cayenne, and simmer for 30 minutes, stirring occasionally. Serve over rice.

Makes 4 servings.

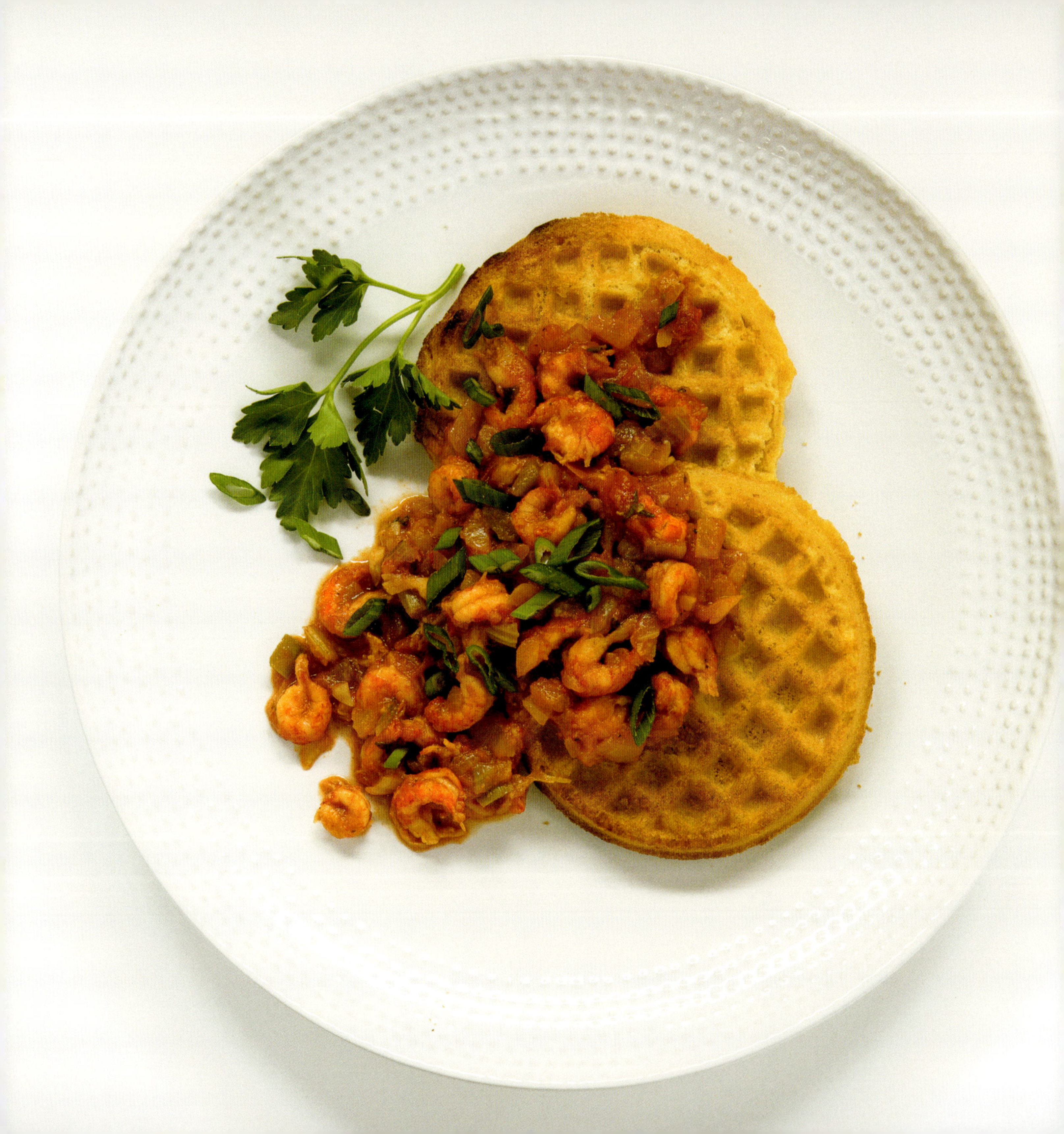

Crawfish Piquante with Rice Waffles

....

We would usually serve this dish with rice, but rice waffles make an interesting change of pace.

¼ cup extra-virgin olive oil
1 medium onion, chopped
1 stalk celery, chopped
1 bell pepper, chopped
4 cloves garlic, diced
2 tablespoons tomato paste
2 tablespoons dark roux
2 cups chicken stock or broth
1 cup crushed tomatoes in puree
1 bay leaf
Coarse salt & freshly ground black pepper
Cayenne
Hot sauce
1 pound crawfish tails
2 tablespoons chopped parsley
2 tablespoons chopped green onion tops

Rice Waffles

2 cups rice flour
2 teaspoons baking powder
¼ teaspoon salt
1 cup milk
2 eggs, lightly beaten
2 tablespoons melted butter

Cook onion, celery, bell pepper and garlic in oil until softened, about 5 minutes. Add tomato paste and roux, stir to combine, and simmer for 5 minutes. Add chicken stock or broth, crushed tomatoes, bay leaf and thyme. Bring to a boil, reduce heat, season to taste with salt, peppers and hot sauce, and simmer, stirring occasionally, for 30 minutes. Add crawfish and simmer for another 30 minutes. Adjust seasonings.

Rice Waffles

Preheat waffle iron. Preheat oven to 275 degrees. Position a rack on a baking sheet and place in oven.

Place dry ingredients in mixing bowl and whisk to combine. Add milk, eggs and melted butter; stir to combine.

Spoon batter on hot waffle iron and cook until crisp and browned. Transfer cooked waffles to baking sheet and keep warm in oven while preparing the remainder.

Serve crawfish over rice waffles, garnished with onion tops and parsley.

Makes 4 or more waffles, depending on size of waffle iron

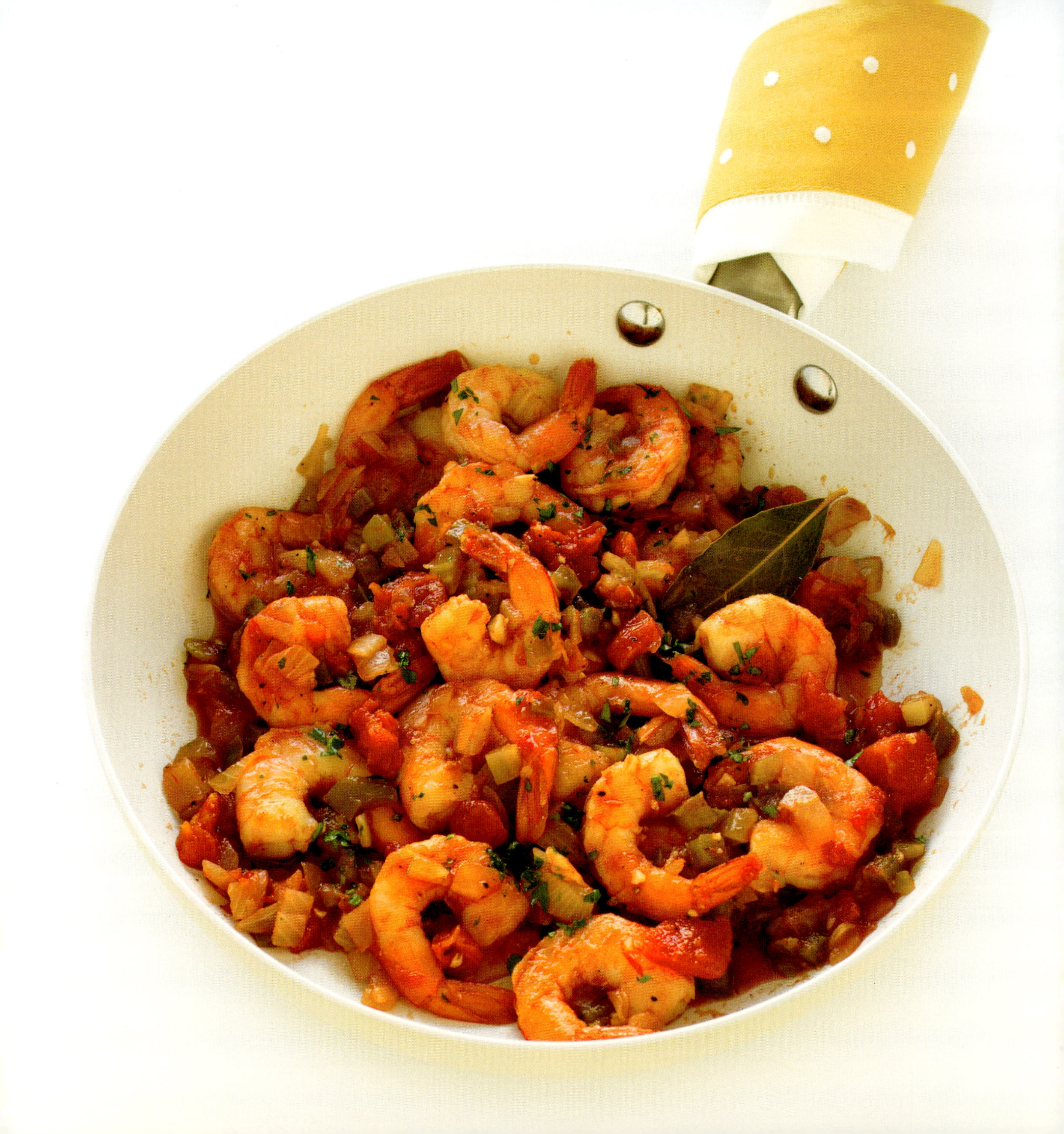

Shrimp Creole Light

A tasty dish that can be prepared quickly, it contains only vegetables, shrimp and seasonings. For additional flavor, you can add ground, dried shrimp.

- 2 medium onions, chopped
- 4 garlic cloves, minced
- 2 stalks celery, chopped
- 2 bell peppers, chopped
- 1 (14.5 oz.) can diced tomatoes
- 2 bay leaves
- Coarse salt & freshly ground black pepper
- Cayenne
- Hot sauce
- 1 pound shrimp, peeled & deveined
- 2 tablespoons chopped parsley

In a large, heavy pot, combine onions, garlic, celery, bell peppers, tomatoes with their juice and bay leaves. Cook on low heat, stirring occasionally, for 30 minutes. Season to taste with salt, peppers and hot sauce. Add shrimp and cook, stirring occasionally, until shrimp turn pink, about 5 minutes. Add parsley and adjust seasonings. Serve over rice.

Makes 4 servings.

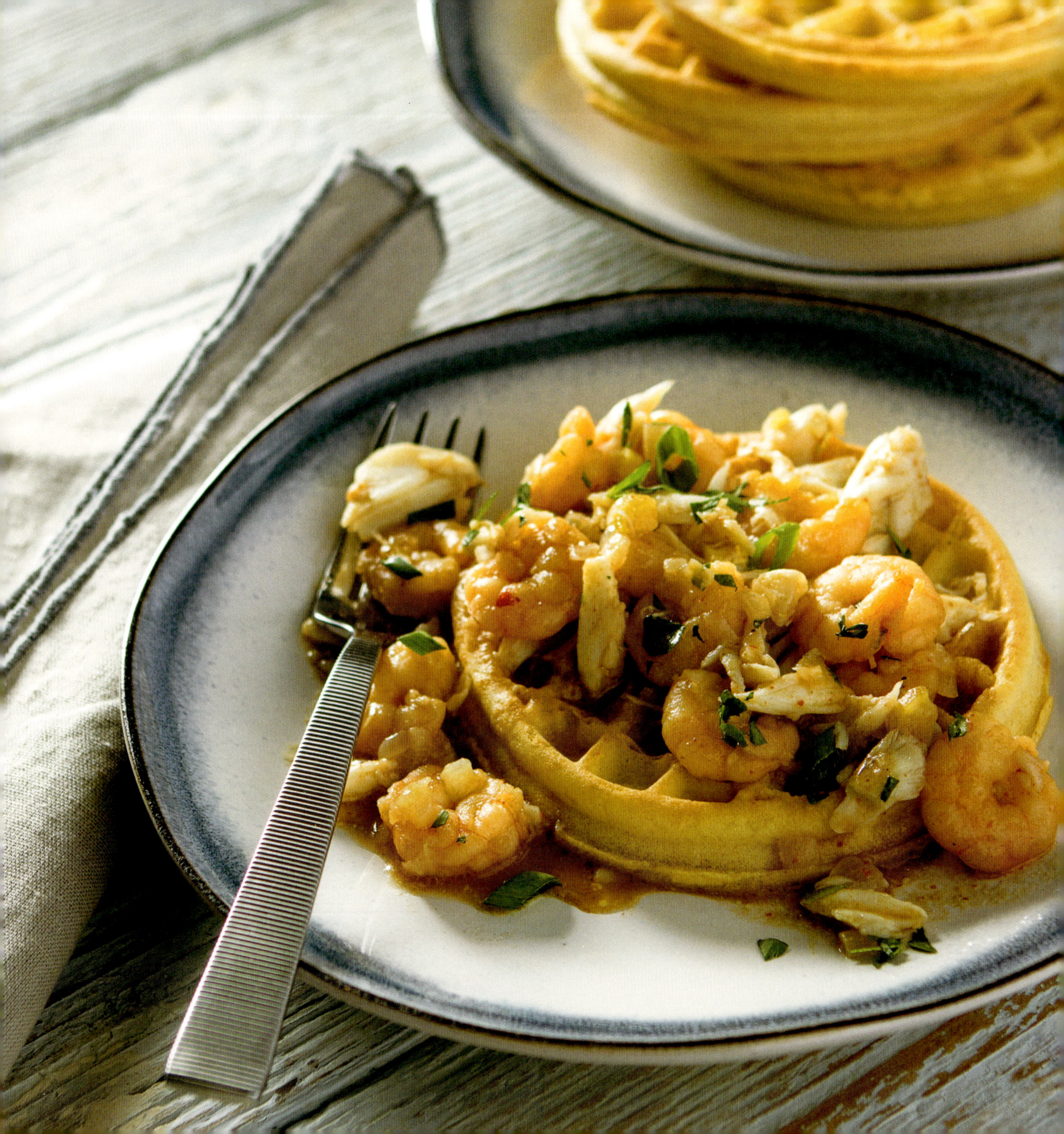

Shrimp & Lump Crabmeat Etouffée with Cornmeal Waffles

Waffles don't have to be reserved for the breakfast table. Prepared without sugar, they can serve as a base for a variety of savory preparations.

- ½ cup butter
- 2 large onions, chopped fine
- 2 stalks celery, chopped fine
- ⅓ cup dry roux
- 2 cups chicken stock or broth
- 2 tablespoons lemon juice
- Coarse salt
- Cayenne pepper
- 1 pound shrimp, peeled & deveined
- 1 pound lump crabmeat
- ¼ cup chopped parsley
- ¼ cup chopped green onion tops

Cornmeal Waffles

- 1 cup cornmeal, preferably stone-ground
- 1 cup all-purpose flour
- ½ teaspoon salt
- 2 teaspoons baking powder
- 1¼ cups milk
- 4 eggs, lightly beaten
- 5 tablespoons melted butter

In a heavy pot over medium heat, melt butter and cook onions and celery, stirring occasionally, until softened, about 5 minutes. Meanwhile, in a small mixing bowl, whisk together cold chicken broth and dry roux until smooth. Add to pot. Bring to a boil, reduce heat and simmer until thickened, about 30 minutes. Add lemon juice. Season to taste with salt and cayenne. Add shrimp and cook until shrimp colors, about 5 minutes. Add lump crabmeat and cook only until crabmeat is heated through. Adjust seasonings. Serve over cornmeal waffles; garnish with parsley and onion tops.

Cornmeal Waffles

Preheat waffle iron. Preheat oven to 275 degrees. Place a rack on a baking sheet and place in oven.

Combine dry ingredients in a bowl and whisk to mix well. Add milk, eggs and melted butter; stir to combine.

Spoon batter on hot waffle iron and cook until crisp and browned. Transfer cooked waffles to baking sheet and keep warm in oven while preparing the remainder.

Makes 6 or more waffles, depending on size of waffle iron.

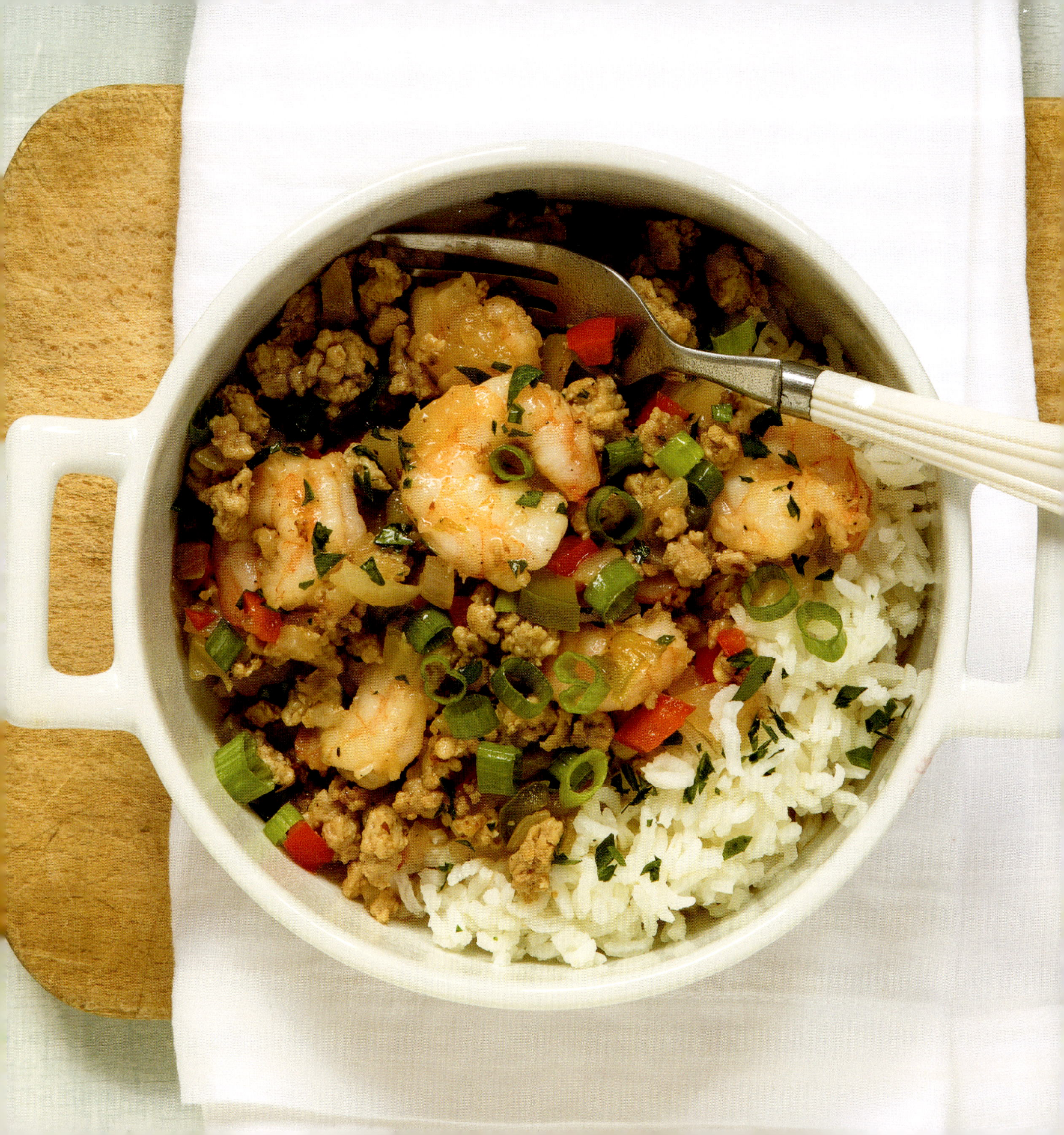

Shrimp & Pork Stew

....

Shrimp and pork have an affinity for one another and are often combined to good effect in Asian cuisines. You could call this a Louisiana version of surf and turf. It is a good example of the adaptability of our shrimp.

2	tablespoons vegetable or olive oil
1	large onion, chopped
4	cloves garlic, chopped
1	rib celery, chopped
1	large green bell pepper, chopped
1	large red bell pepper, chopped
1	pound ground pork
1	cup water
2	tablespoons dry roux
	Coarse salt & freshly ground black pepper
	Cayenne
	Hot sauce
1	pound shrimp, peeled & deveined
2	tablespoons chopped parsley
2	tablespoons chopped green onion tops

In a large pot, cook onion, garlic, celery and bell peppers in oil, stirring occasionally, until softened, about 5 minutes. Add pork and cook, stirring frequently, until browned, about 5-10 minutes.

Meanwhile, in a small pot, bring water to a boil and whisk in roux until dissolved; add to large pot and simmer, stirring occasionally, for 10 minutes. Season to taste with salt, peppers and hot sauce. Add shrimp and simmer, stirring occasionally, until shrimp turn pink, about 5 minutes. Adjust seasonings, add parsley and onion tops. Serve over steamed rice.

Makes 4 or more servings.

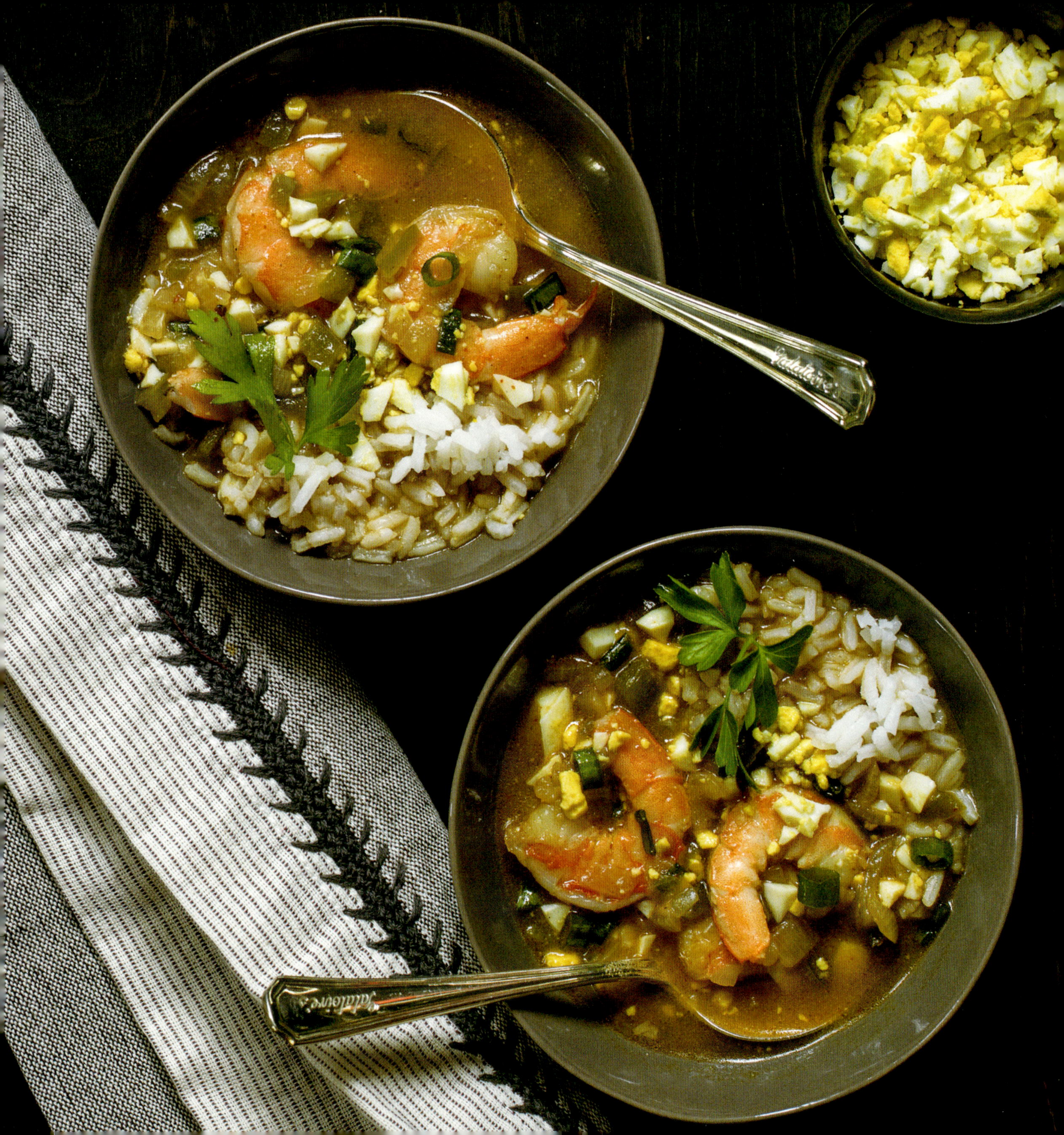

Shrimp & Egg Stew

If you have heads-on shrimp, you can replace the chicken stock or broth in this recipe with shrimp stock made by simmering the heads and shells in water. Seasoning preferences vary greatly here. Some like the stew spicy, others prefer mild seasonings to accentuate the sweetness of the shrimp. I am in the latter camp.

2	tablespoons extra-virgin olive oil
1	onion, chopped
1	bell pepper, chopped
2	cloves garlic, minced
2	cups chicken stock or broth
2	tablespoons dry roux
2	pounds shrimp, peeled & deveined
4	eggs
	Coarse salt & freshly ground black pepper
	Cayenne
¼	cup chopped parsley
¼	cup chopped green onion tops

In a large, heavy pot over medium heat, cook onions, bell pepper, and garlic in oil, stirring occasionally, until softened, about 5 minutes. Combine roux and stock in a mixing bowl and whisk to dissolve roux. Add contents to pot. Bring to a boil, reduce heat, cover and simmer for 10 minutes. Add shrimp and simmer, covered, for 10 minutes.

Meanwhile, in another pot, cover eggs with water, bring to a boil, cover, turn off heat and let sit for 10 minutes. Drain and place under running cold water to cool. Peel eggs and chop finely.

Add eggs to shrimp mixture, season to taste with salt, black pepper and cayenne; simmer for 5 minutes. Add parsley and green onion tops and serve with steamed rice.

Makes 4 servings.

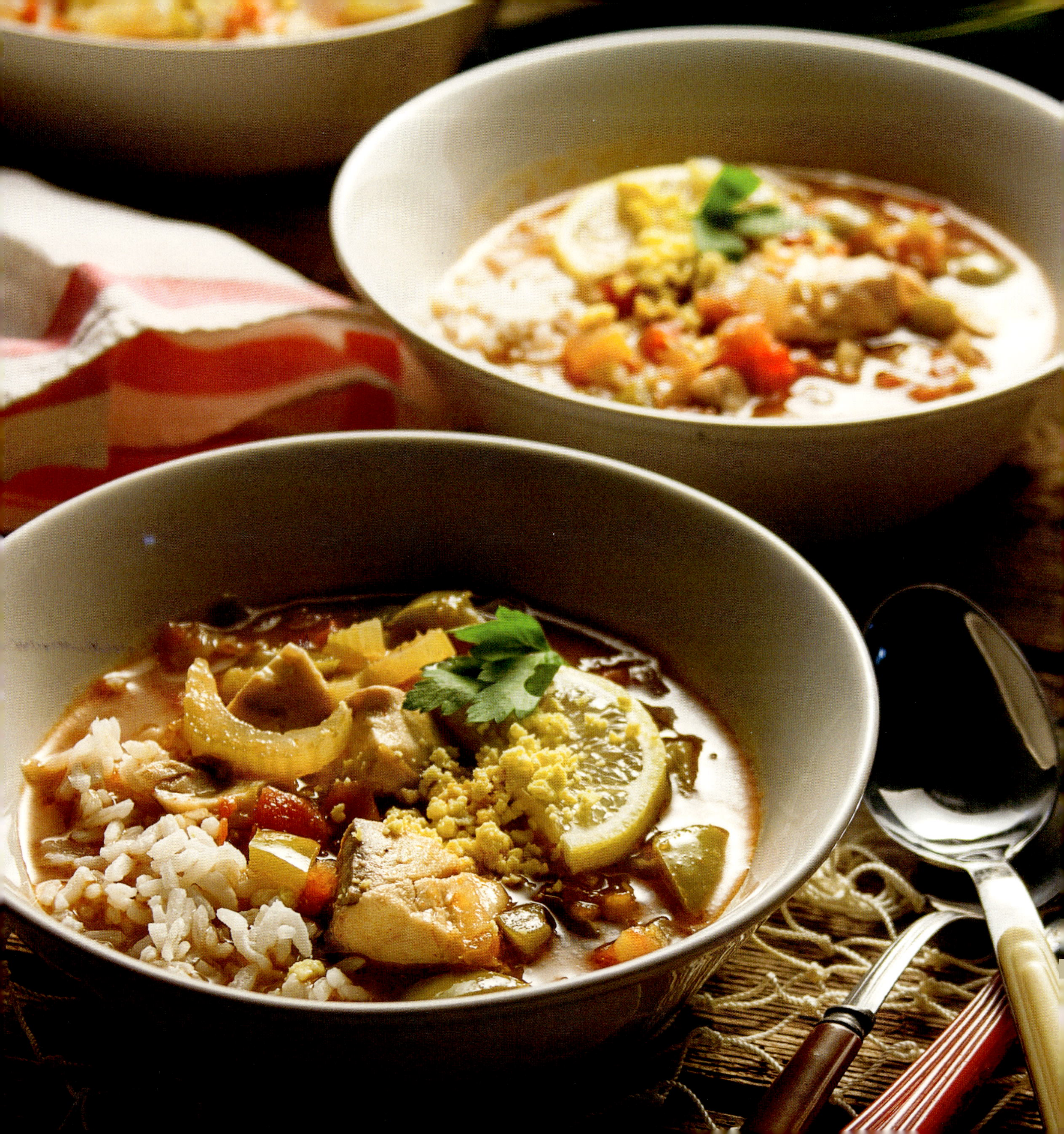

Courtbouillon

In French cuisine, "court bouillon" is a flavored broth in which seafood is poached. In Louisiana, a courtbouillon (one word) is a dish of fish cooked in a tomato gravy.

3	tablespoons extra-virgin olive oil
1	large onion, chopped
1	large bell pepper, chopped
1	stalk celery, chopped
2	cloves garlic, minced
3	cups chicken stock or broth
2	tablespoons dry roux
1	cup dry white wine
1	(14.5 oz.) can diced tomatoes
2	tablespoons tomato paste
2	bay leaves
½	teaspoon dried thyme leaves
¼	teaspoon ground allspice
	Coarse salt & freshly ground black pepper
	Cayenne
2	pounds redfish or other firm-fleshed fish
2	tablespoons lemon juice
¼	cup chopped parsley
½	cup chopped green onion tops

In a large, heavy pot over medium heat, cook onions, bell pepper, celery and garlic in oil, stirring occasionally, until softened, about 5 minutes. Combine roux and stock in a mixing bowl and whisk to dissolve roux. Add contents to pot. Add wine, tomatoes with their juice, tomato paste, bay leaves, thyme and allspice to pot. Bring to a boil and season to taste with salt, black pepper and cayenne. Simmer, stirring occasionally, for about 45 minutes. Cut fish into 2-inch chunks. Add to pot and cook until fish flakes easily with a fork, about 10 minutes. Add lemon juice and adjust seasonings. Add parsley and green onion tops. Serve over steamed rice.

Makes 4 or more servings.

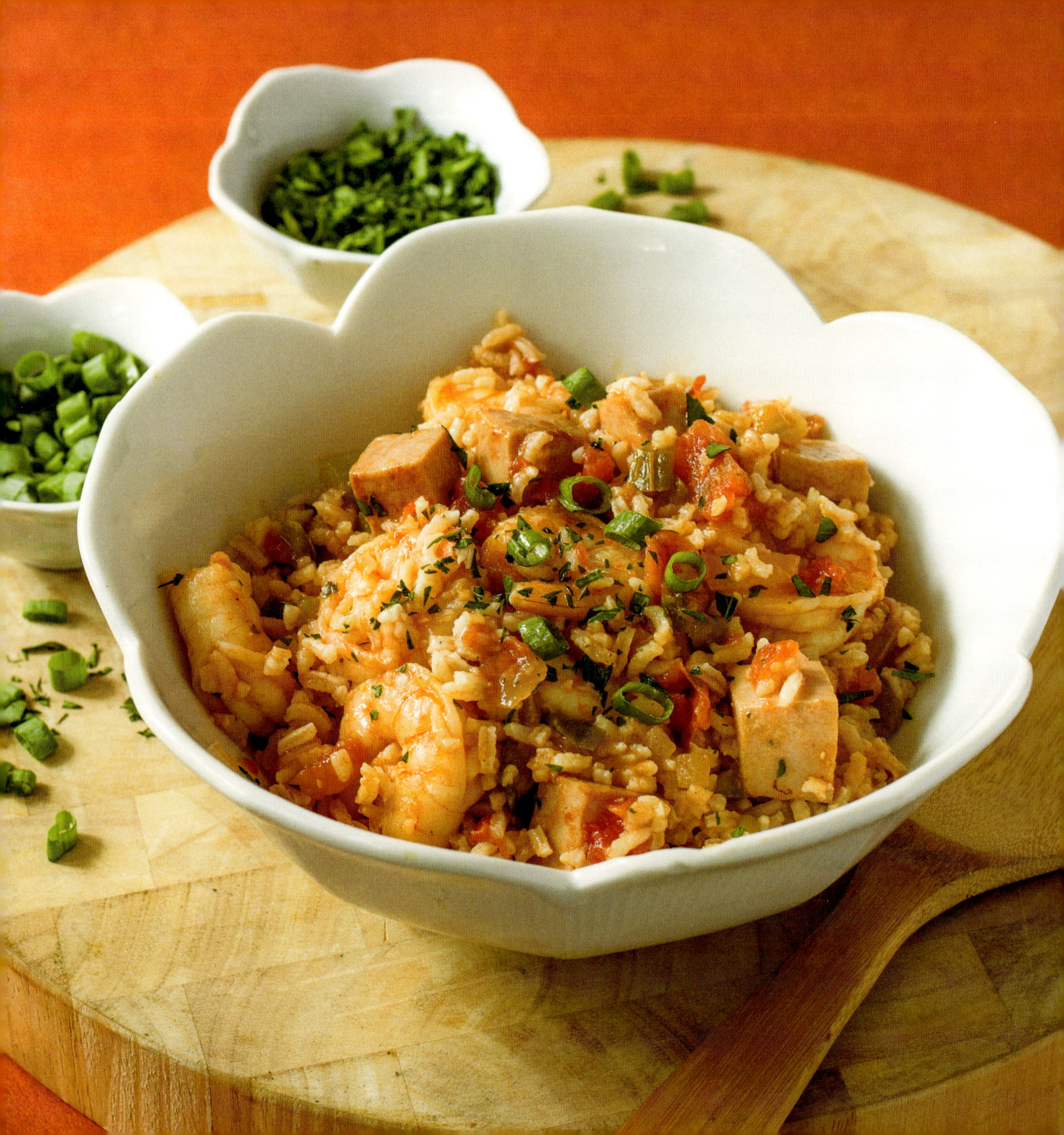

Jambalayas & Rice

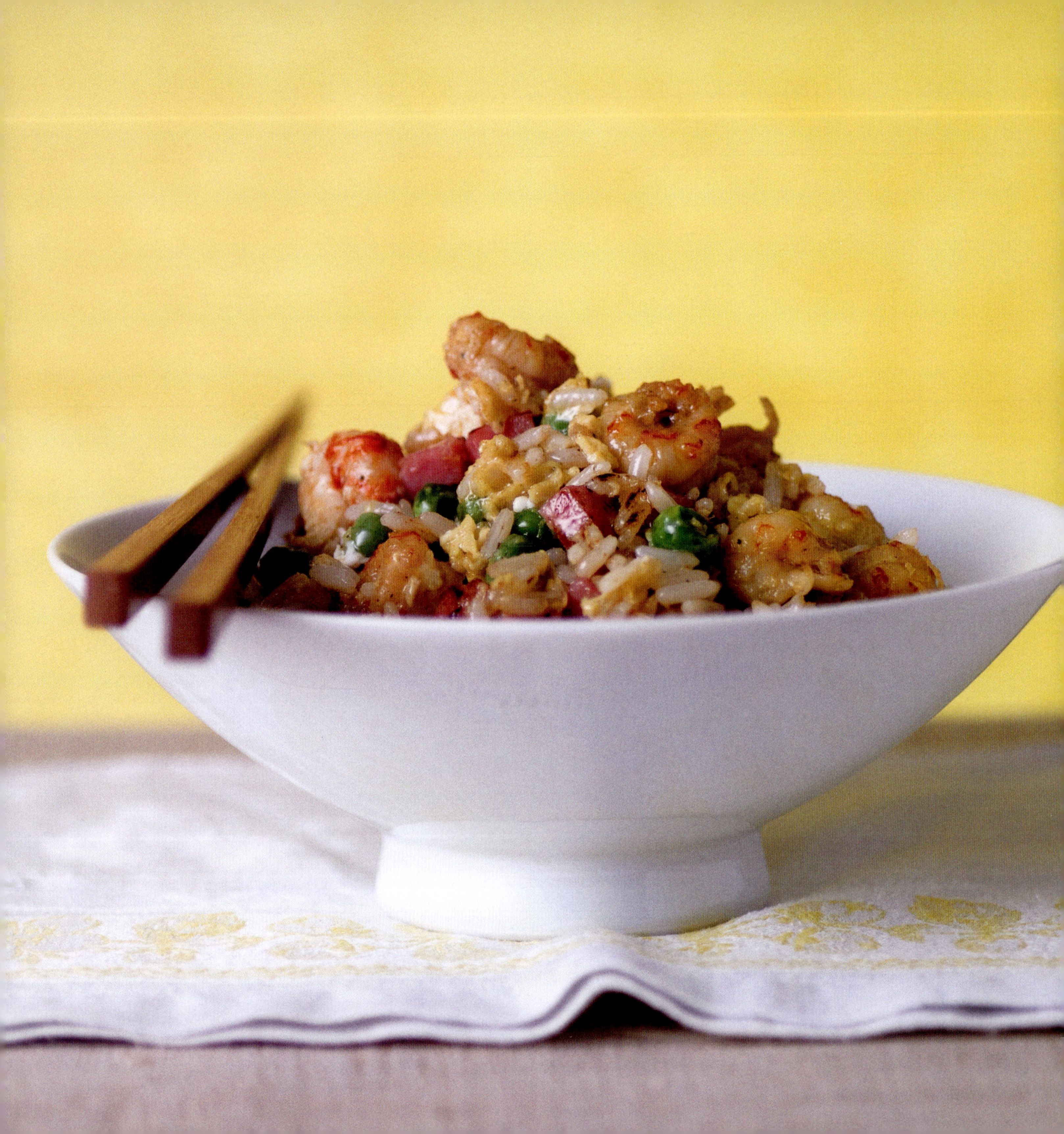

Crawfish Fried Rice

....

Since you'll get the best results with cooked rice that has been refrigerated, this is an excellent way to use leftovers. To prevent sticking and to assure a non-greasy result, make sure the oil is very hot before adding the rice.

4	cups cold cooked rice
1	pound crawfish tails
	Hot sauce
	Cajun/Creole seasoning
2	tablespoons vegetable oil
1	cup frozen green peas
½	cup diced ham
2	eggs, well beaten
	Coarse salt

Using a fork, separate grains of rice. Generously season crawfish with hot sauce and creole seasoning. In a wok or large skillet, over high heat, heat oil until it shimmers. Add rice and stir-fry for 1 minute. Add crawfish, peas and ham, and stir-fry for 5 minutes. Add egg and stir-fry for another minute. Season to taste with salt.

Makes 4 servings.

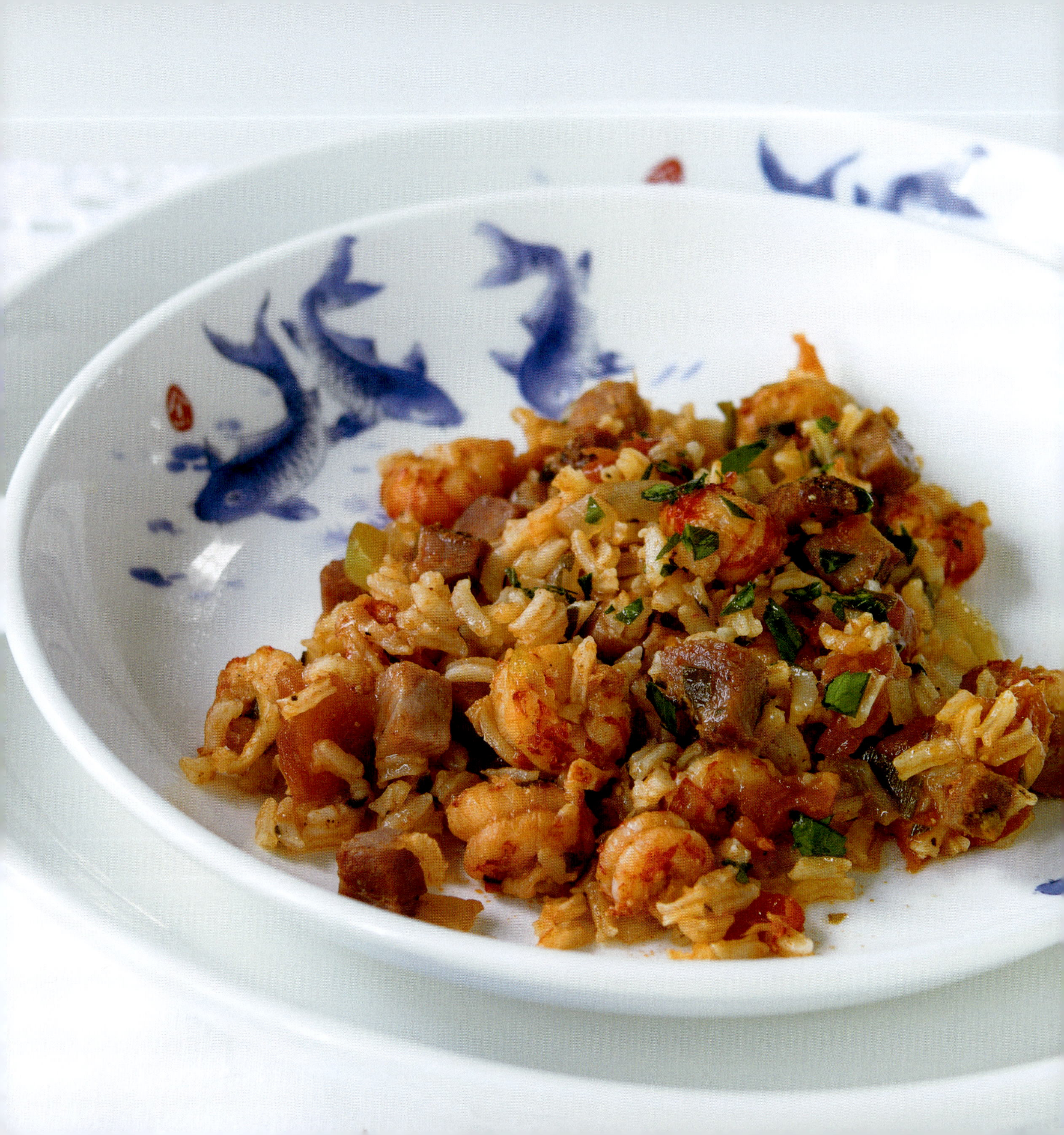

Crawfish & Tasso Jambalaya

Crawfish and pork are a felicitous combination, particularly when the pork has been seasoned and smoked to produce tasso, the Cajun charcuterie specialty. With the addition of rice, you have a Cajun trifecta. In Acadiana, most cooks do not use tomatoes in their jambalaya, so their addition here is a personal preference.

- 2 tablespoons vegetable or olive oil
- 1 medium onion, diced
- 1 rib celery, diced
- 1 medium bell pepper, diced
- 2 cloves garlic, minced
- 1 cup diced tasso
- 1 pound peeled crawfish tails
- 1 (14.5 oz.) can diced tomatoes
- 1½ cups chicken stock or broth
- 1 teaspoon Cajun/Creole seasoning
- ¼ teaspoon hot sauce
- 2 tablespoons chopped parsley
- ¼ cup chopped green onion tops
- 1 cup rice

Heat oil in a heavy pot, add onion, celery, bell pepper, garlic and tasso, and cook until vegetables are softened, about 5 minutes. Add crawfish tails, tomatoes with juice, chicken stock or broth, Cajun/Creole seasoning, hot sauce, parsley and green onion tops, and bring to a boil. Add rice, cover, reduce heat and simmer until liquid is absorbed and rice is tender, about 20-25 minutes. Adjust seasonings.

Makes 4 servings.

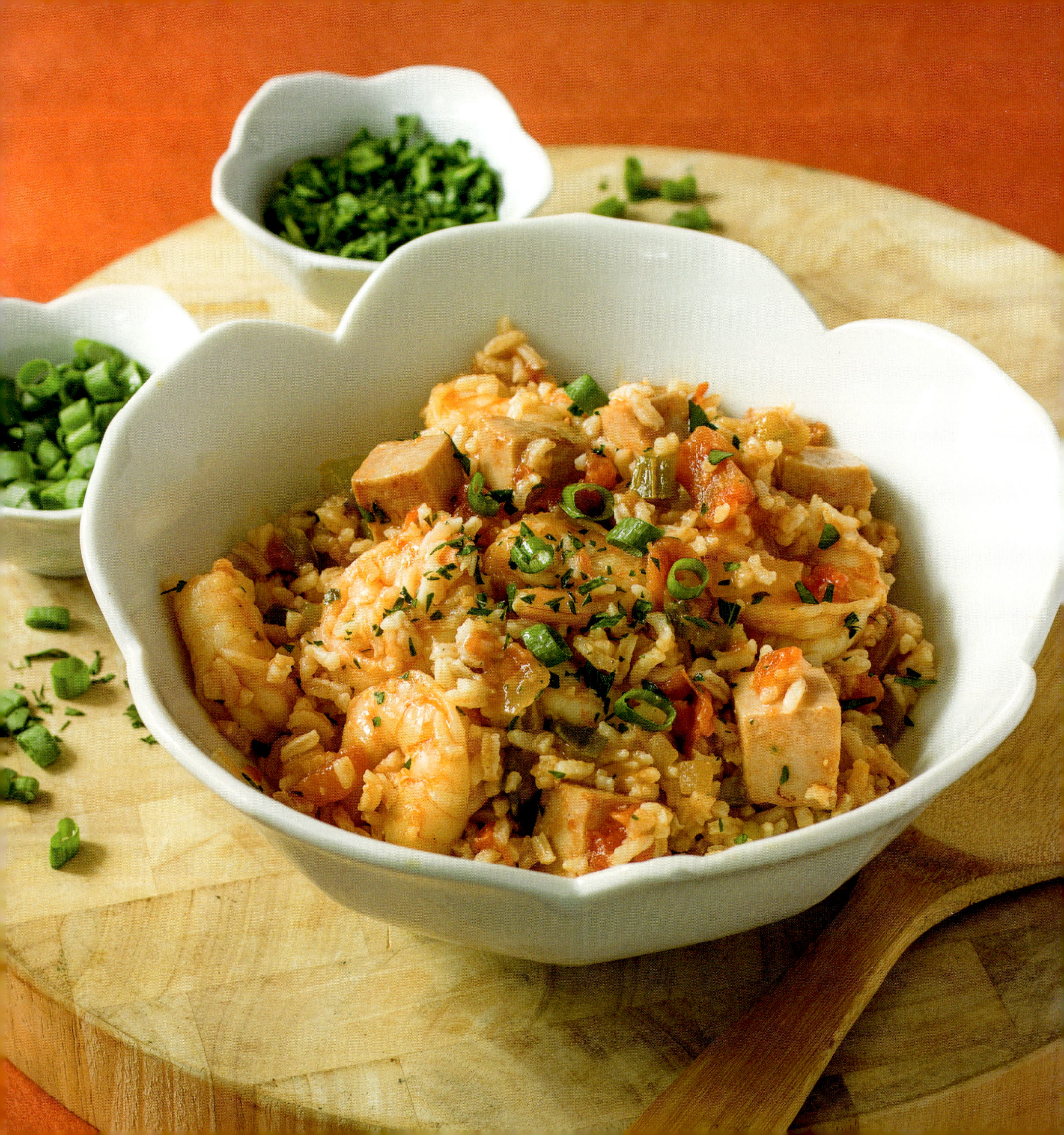

Shrimp & Ham Jambalaya

....

Shrimp, ham and tomatoes are commonly combined in many jambalayas prepared by New Orleans cooks.

2	tablespoons vegetable or olive oil
1	medium onion, diced
1	stalk celery, diced
1	medium bell pepper, diced
2	cloves garlic, minced
1	cup cubed ham
1	pound shrimp, peeled & deveined
1	(14.5 oz.) can diced tomatoes
1½	cups chicken stock or broth
1	teaspoon Cajun/Creole seasoning
¼	teaspoon hot sauce
2	tablespoons chopped parsley
¼	cup chopped green onion tops
1	cup rice

Heat oil in a heavy pot, add onion, celery, bell pepper, garlic and ham, and cook until vegetables are softened, about 5 minutes. Add shrimp, tomatoes with juice, chicken stock or broth, Cajun/Creole seasoning, hot sauce, parsley and onion tops and bring to a boil. Add rice, cover, reduce heat and simmer until liquid is absorbed and rice is tender, about 20-25 minutes. Adjust sesonings.

Makes 4 servings.

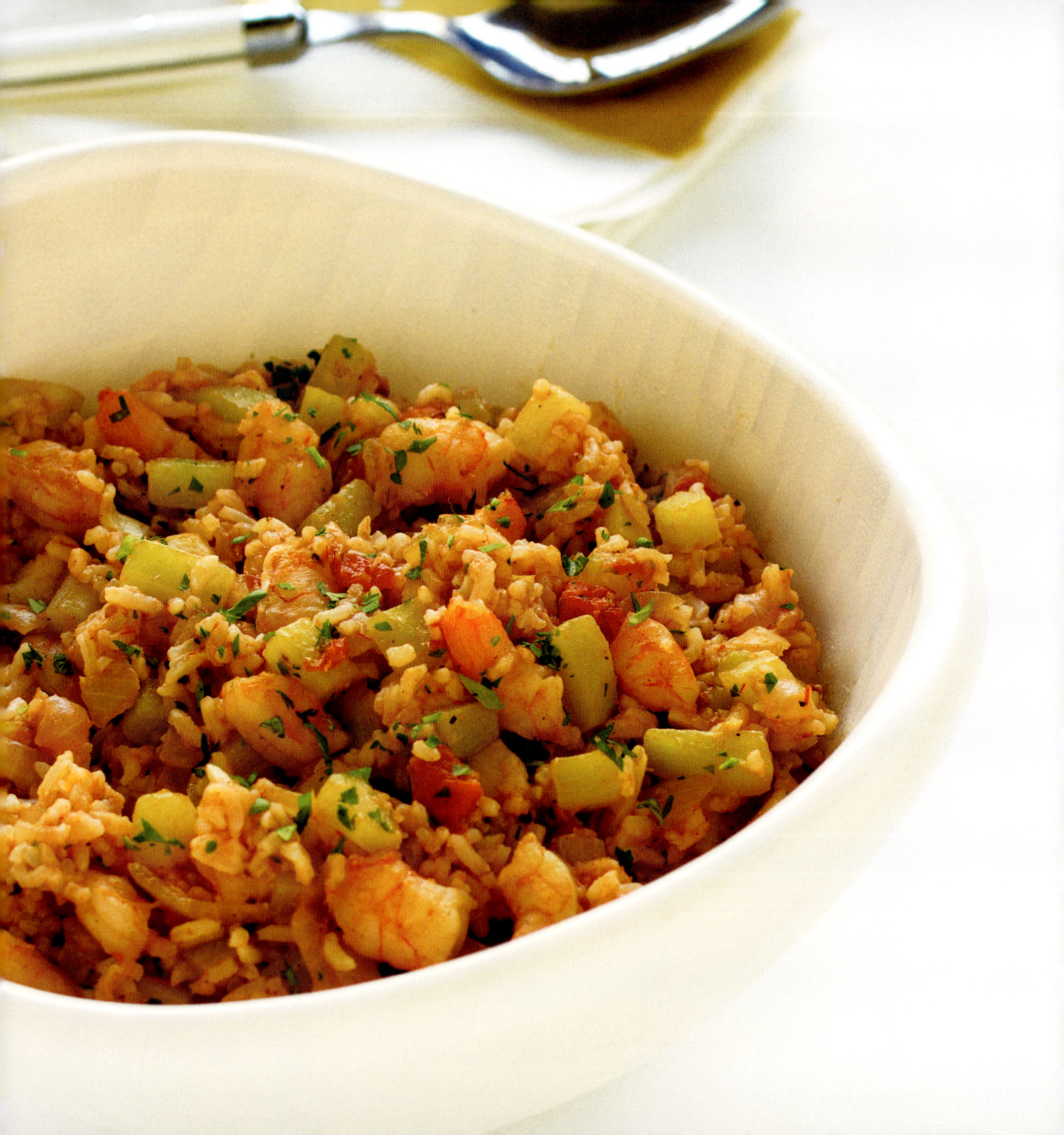

Shrimp & Mirliton Rice Dressing

Recipes often call for discarding the mirliton seeds, but they are actually quite tasty, with an almond-like flavor.

- 2 small mirlitons, peeled & chopped
- 1 medium onion, chopped
- 1 cup chicken stock or broth
- 1 cup crushed tomatoes
- 1 pound shrimp, peeled, deveined & chopped
- 4 tablespoons ground, dried shrimp
- 3 cups cooked rice
- Cajun/Creole seasoning
- Coarse salt & freshly ground black pepper
- Hot sauce
- 2 tablespoons chopped parsley

Combine mirlitons, onion and stock or broth in a heavy pot, bring to a boil, reduce heat, cover and simmer until vegetables are tender, about 10 minutes. Add tomatoes, shrimp and ground, dried shrimp, and cook, stirring occasionally, until shrimp are tender, about 5 minutes. Add rice and stir to combine. Season to taste with Cajun/Creole seasoning, salt, pepper and hot sauce. Add chopped parsley.

Makes about 6 servings.

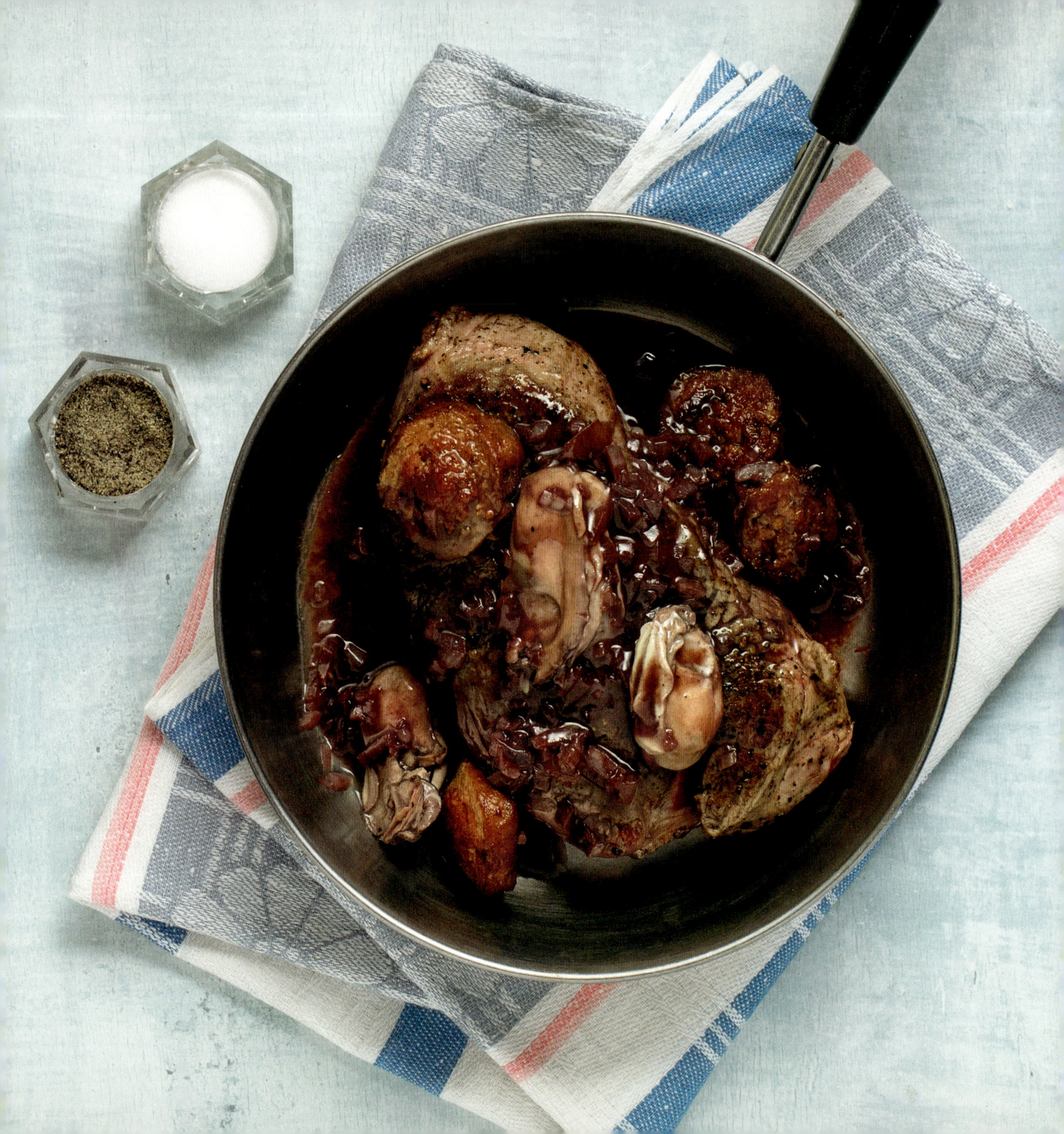

Pan Fried, Grilled, Broiled & Boiled

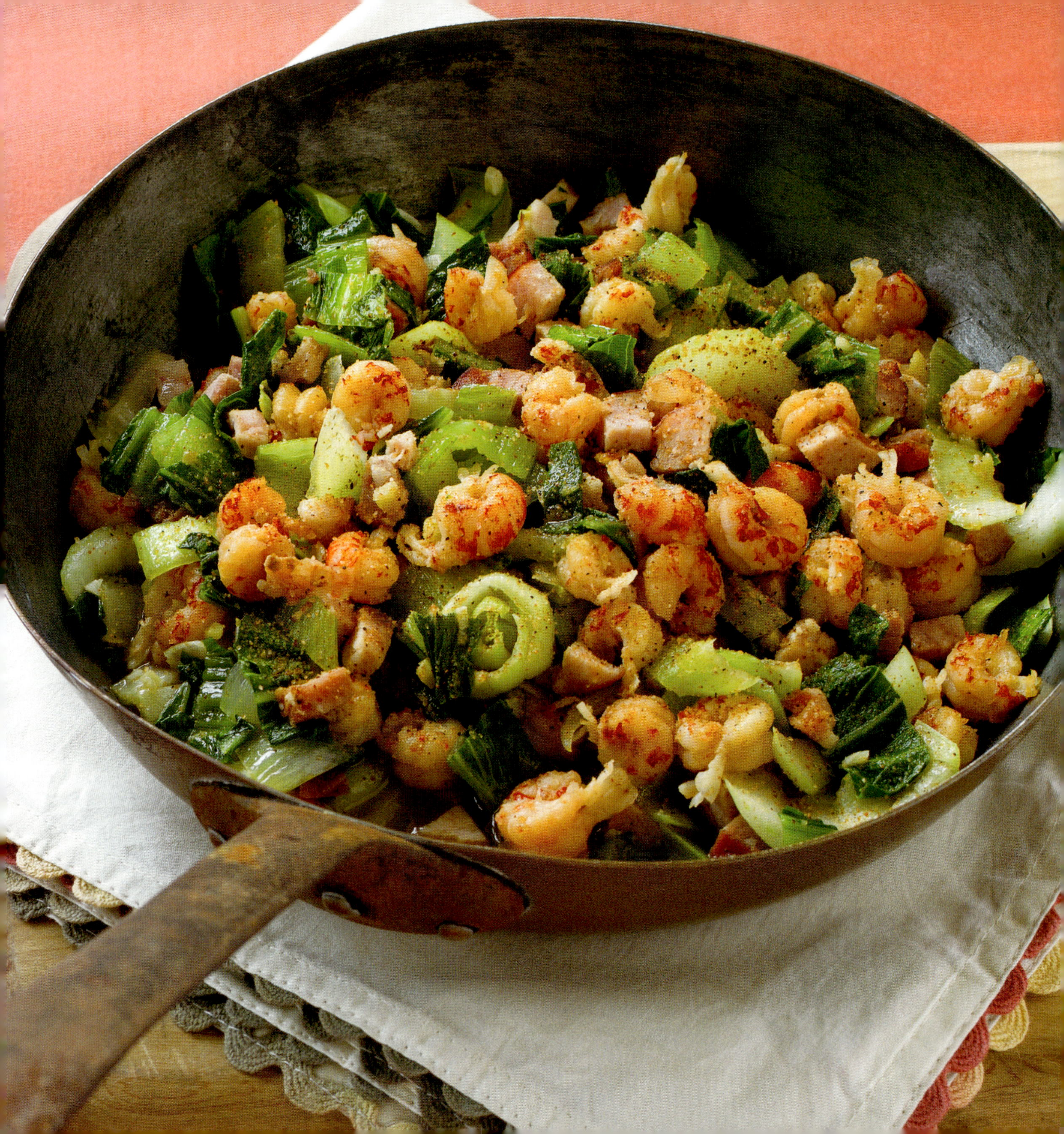

Stir-Fried Crawfish with Tasso & Bok Choy

This dish, which requires little prep and cooks quickly, is ideal for a busy weeknight.

1	tablespoon vegetable oil
1	tablespoon minced garlic
1	tablespoon minced ginger root
½	cup cubed tasso
1	cup peeled crawfish tails
4	cups chopped bok choy
½	cup chicken stock or broth
	Cajun/Creole seasoning

Heat wok or large skillet over high heat. Add oil and heat. Add garlic and ginger root and stir quickly until fragrant. Add tasso and stir briefly. Add crawfish and stir. Add bok choy and stir. Add chicken stock or broth and cook, while stirring and tossing, until bok choy softens. Season to taste with Cajun/Creole seasoning. Serve with steamed rice.

Makes 4 servings.

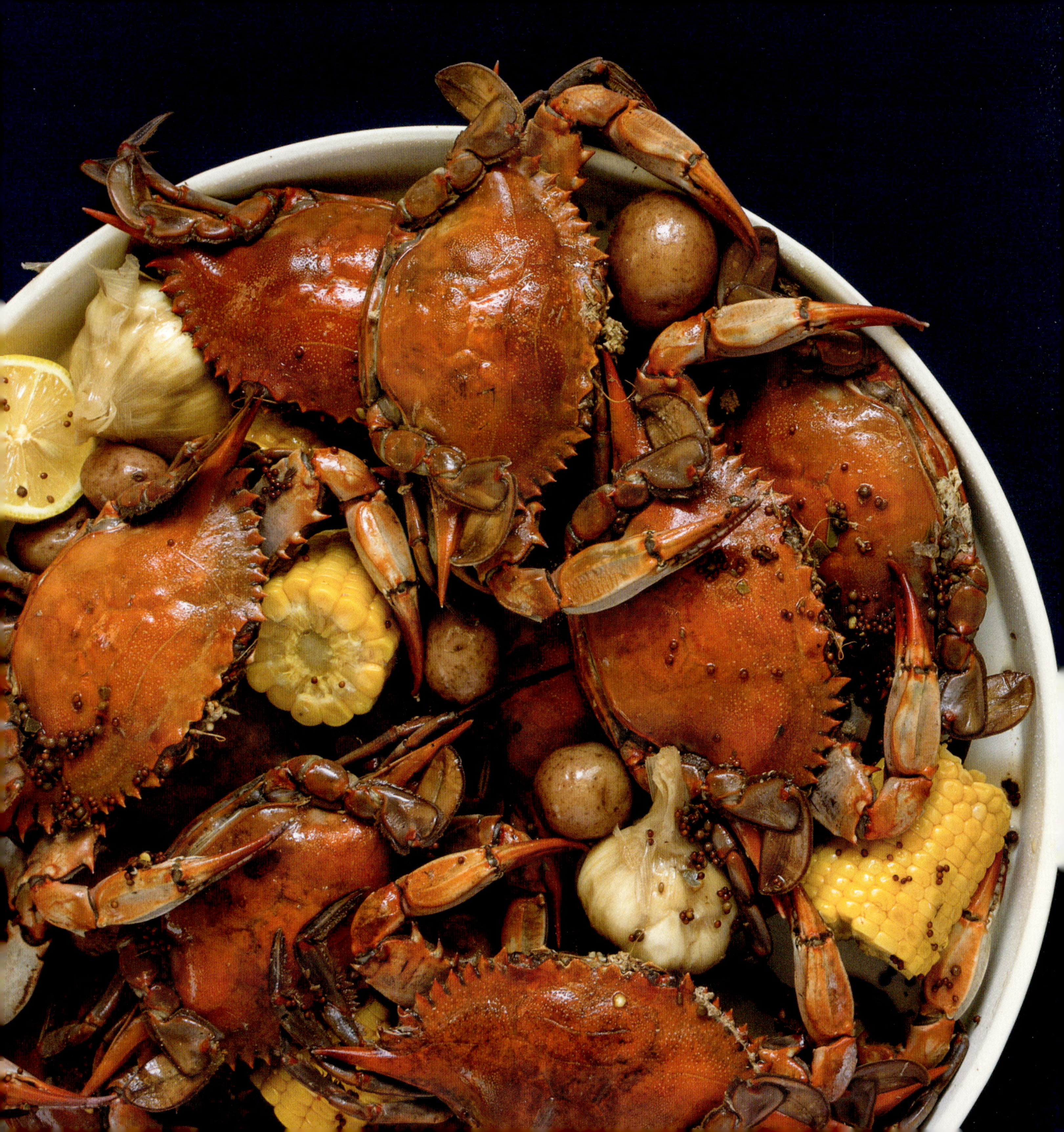

Boiled Crabs

....

The 1901 edition of "The Picayune's Creole Cook Book" included instructions for eating boiled crabs with a knife and fork, "without once using the fingers." That must have been quite a feat, and it certainly bears no resemblance to the modern crab boil, where everyone rolls up their sleeves and has at it. Judging from the old recipe, there was much less hot pepper involved in the boil than is customary today.

There are dozens of brands of crab boil on the market, and they very greatly in the amount of red pepper they contain, so it's advisable to start with the amount recommended on the package and add additional to taste. You'll need a large pot with a removable basket and a heat source, usually a propane burner. Into this pot will go water, salt, crab boil, halved lemons, garlic, and any other spices, such as cayenne pepper, you wish. Bring the pot to a boil and let it boil for about 10 minutes. Taste the water and add additional crab boil and other seasonings, as desired. If you're cooking smoked sausage, corn or small red potatoes, add them to the pot. When the water comes back to a boil, add the live crabs and cook for 10 minutes. Turn off the heat, dump in a bag of ice to stop the cooking, and let the crabs soak in the water for 10 minutes to absorb the seasonings. Lift out the basket, turn out the crabs on a newspaper covered table, and dig in, no forks needed, though knives are useful for cracking the claws.

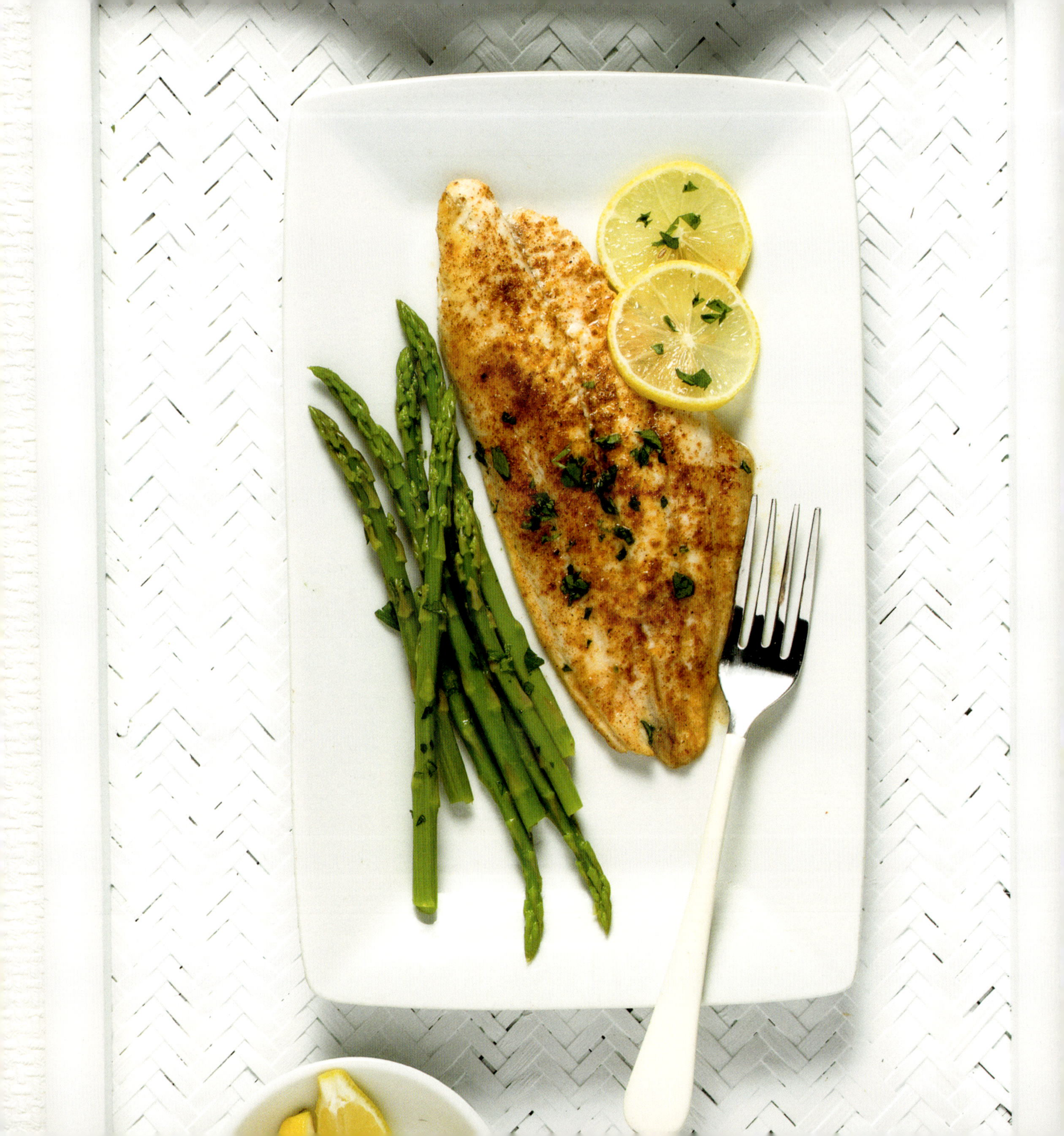

Broiled Catfish

Fried catfish is a staple of menus throughout Louisiana, but in recent years the option of ordering broiled catfish is increasingly common.

- 4 large catfish fillets
- ¼ cup dry white wine
- 2 tablespoons melted butter
- Cajun/Creole seasoning
- 1 tablespoon chopped parsley
- Lemon wedges

Preheat broiler. Grease a rimmed, heavy-duty baking sheet with some of the butter. Place catfish on pan, pour wine over fish, drizzle with butter and sprinkle with Cajun/Creole seasoning. Broil until fish flakes easily with a fork. Transfer fish to serving plates and spoon over pan drippings. Sprinkle with chopped parsley and serve with lemon wedges.

Makes 4 servings.

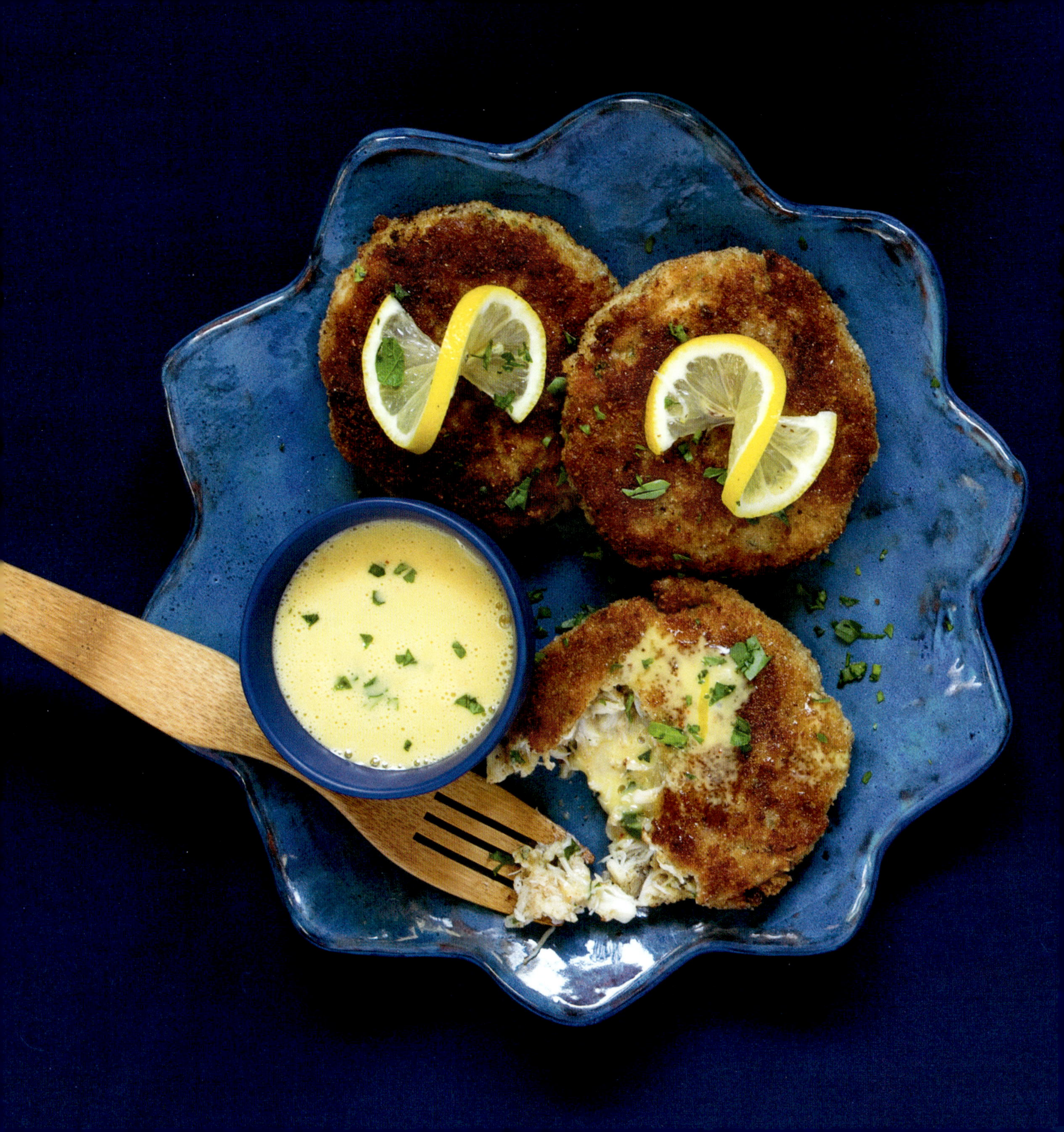

Crab Cakes with Lemon Mayonnaise

Too often, crab cakes suffer from an overabundance of breadcrumbs. A crab cake should contain just enough binding to hold it together; the slight pressure of a diner's fork should cause it to crumble. If you wish, you can use a mixture of lump and claw crabmeat in this recipe.

- 1 pound lump crabmeat, picked over
- 1 teaspoon Cajun/Creole seasoning
- 2 tablespoons freshly squeezed lemon juice
- 1 tablespoon chopped parsley
- 1 tablespoon chopped green onion tops
- 1 egg, lightly beaten
- ½ cup breadcrumbs

For Frying
- ¼ cup olive oil
- ¼ cup flour
- 1 egg, lightly beaten
- ½ cup breadcrumbs

Lemon Mayonnaise
- 2 egg yolks
- ¼ teaspoon salt
- 1 tablespoon freshly squeezed lemon juice
- ½ cup extra-virgin olive oil
- 1 teaspoon finely-grated lemon zest
- Cayenne

Place crabmeat in a mixing bowl. Add Cajun/Creole seasoning, lemon juice, parsley, green onion tops, egg and breadcrumbs. Mix gently with a fork, being careful not to break up crabmeat. Form mixture into 4 cakes.

In a large skillet, heat olive oil on medium heat. When oil is hot, dredge crawfish cakes in flour, then egg, then breadcrumbs. Fry until nicely browned, about 4 minutes; turn and cook on the other side until browned, about 2 minutes. Drain on absorbent paper. Serve with Lemon Mayonnaise.

Makes 4 servings.

Lemon Mayonnaise
In a mixing bowl, beat egg yolks, salt and lemon juice with a wire whisk until pale yellow and creamy. Continue beating, while slowly adding olive oil, a drop at a time in the beginning. As the mixture emulsifies, increase slightly the amount of oil you're adding, while continuing to whisk, until all the oil has been added. Add lemon zest and cayenne to taste, and whisk to incorporate. Adjust seasoning.

Makes about ½ cup.

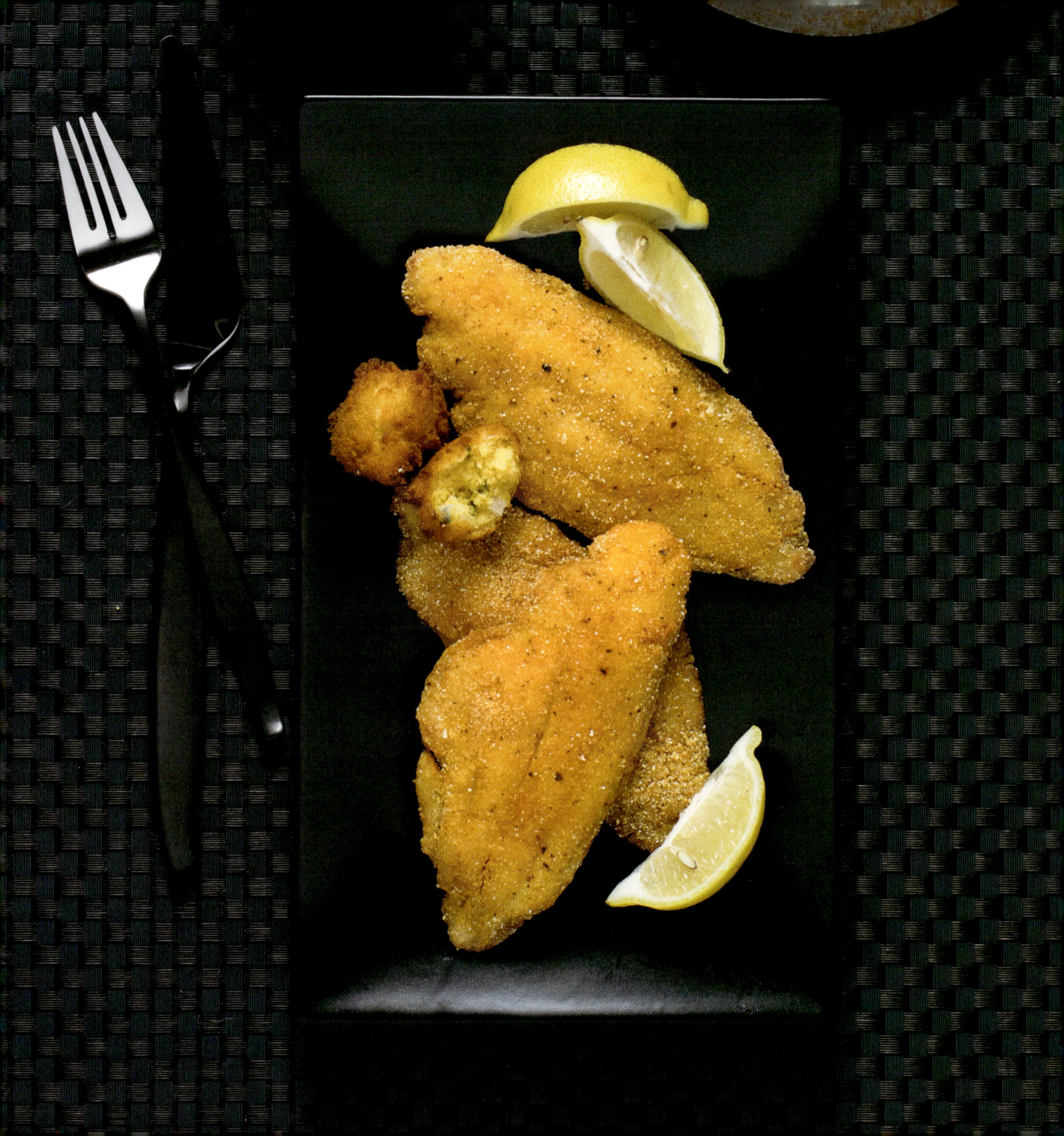

Fried Catfish

Fish breaded with cornmeal will often be grainy. Corn flour, which has a finer texture, is a better choice. If you can't find corn flour labelled as such, unseasoned Fish-Fri is the same thing.

- 2 cups milk
- 2 teaspoons hot sauce
- 2 cups corn flour
- 1 teaspoon coarse salt
- ½ teaspoon freshly ground black pepper
- ½ teaspoon cayenne
- 2 pounds thin catfish fillets
- Cooking oil
- Lemon wedges

Heat oil in fryer or deep pot to 375 degrees. Combine milk and hot sauce in a large bowl. Add catfish to milk. Combine corn flour, salt and peppers in another container. When oil is at proper temperature, remove a filet from milk, shake off excess, dredge in corn flour and drop in the fryer. Repeat with additional catfish, being careful not to overcrowd fryer. Cook until crispy. Remove cooked catfish from fryer and drain. Repeat until all the fish is cooked. Serve with lemon wedges.

Makes 4 servings.

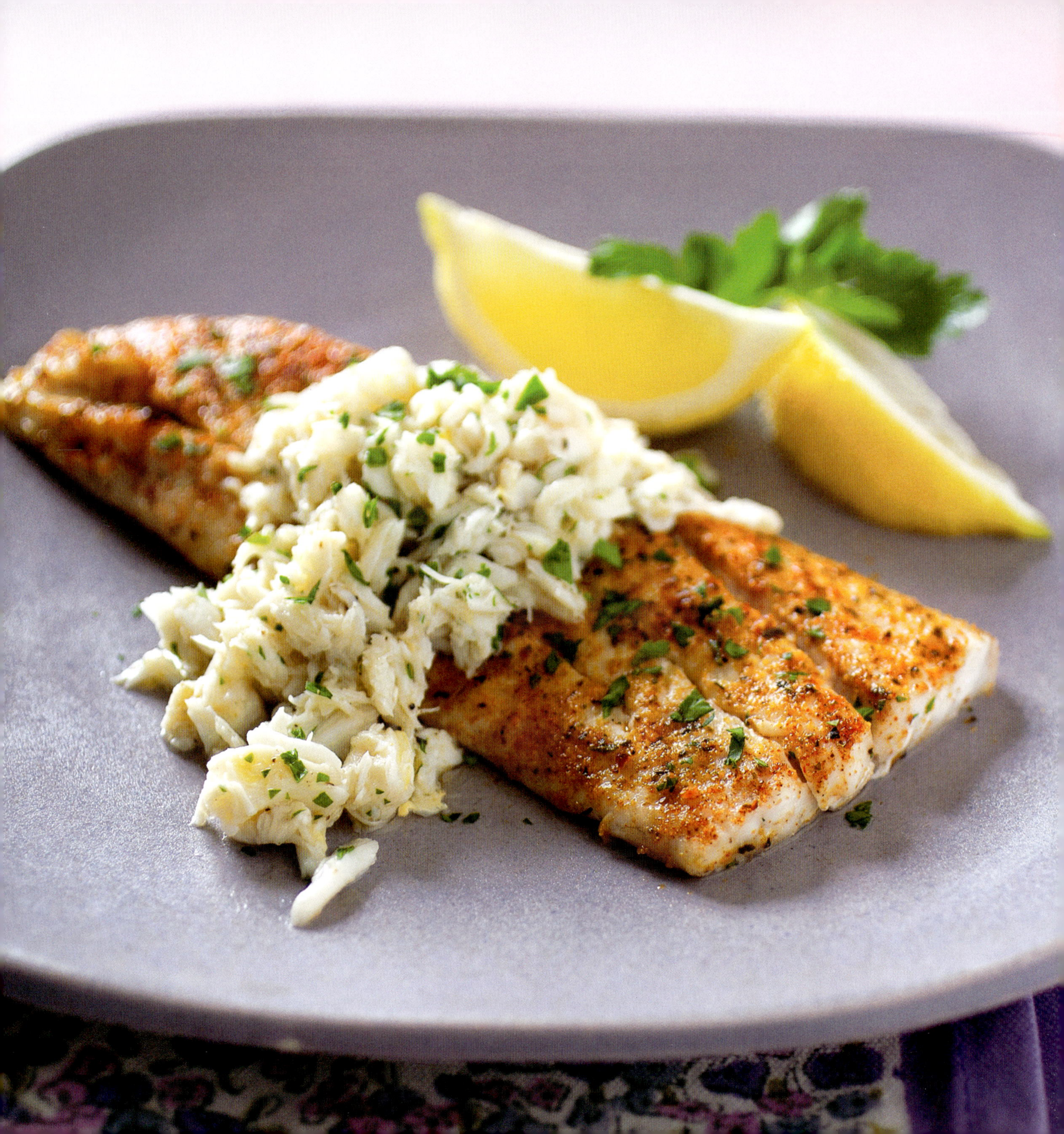

Gulf Fish with Crabmeat

There's not much that can top this preparation. Jumbo lump crabmeat is preferred, but price may dictate white crabmeat.

- 3 tablespoons butter
- 4 Gulf fish fillets, such as redfish or black drum
- ¼ cup dry white wine
- Cajun/Creole seasoning
- 1 pound lump or white crabmeat
- 2 teaspoons freshly squeezed lemon juice
- 1 tablespoon chopped parsley
- Lemon wedges

Preheat broiler. Grease a rimmed, heavy-duty baking sheet with some of the butter. Place fillets on baking sheet and pour over white wine. Season fillets to taste with Cajun/Creole seasoning and divide butter among them. Broil until fish flakes easily with a fork.

Carefully tip baking sheet into a large, nonreactive skillet to drain liquid. Place skillet over high heat, and keep fish warm while preparing crabmeat and sauce. Boil liquid in skillet until it becomes syrupy. Add crabmeat and lemon juice and cook only until crabmeat is heated through. Divide fish fillets among warm serving plates; spoon over crabmeat and sauce. Sprinkle with chopped parsley and serve with lemon wedges.

Makes 4 servings.

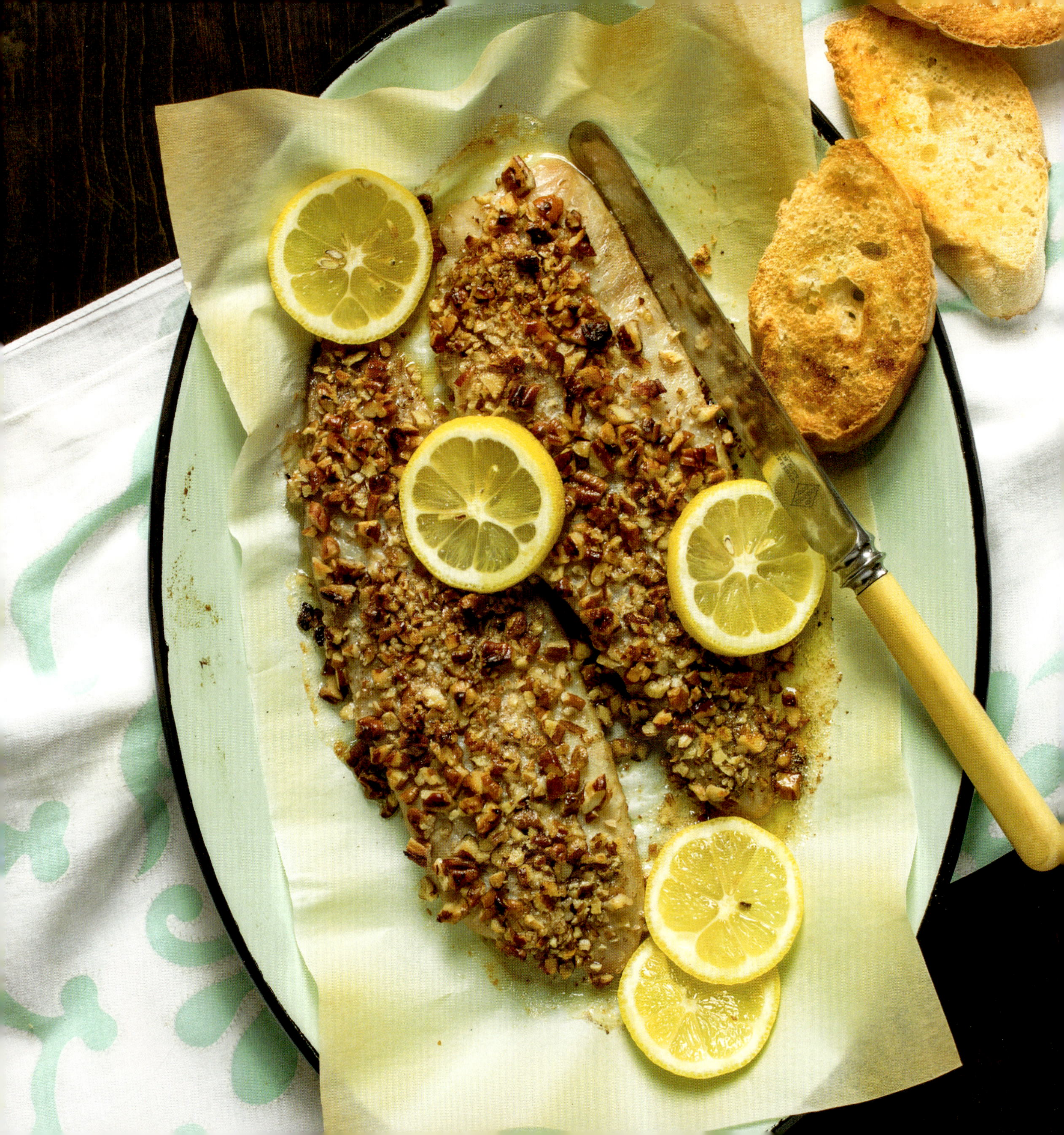

Pan Fried, Grilled, Broiled & Boiled

Pecan Crusted Trout

....

The rich nuttiness of butter and pecans offers a pleasing contrast to the trout.

4	*speckled trout fillets*
	Coarse salt
⅓	*cup chopped pecans*
2	*tablespoons melted butter*
	Lemon wedges

Preheat oven to 450 degrees. Grease a rimmed, heavy-duty baking sheet with some of the butter. Place fillets on baking sheet, season with salt and divide chopped pecans among them, pressing pecans into the fillets. Drizzle melted butter over the fish and bake until they flake easily with a fork. Serve with lemon wedges.

Makes 4 servings.

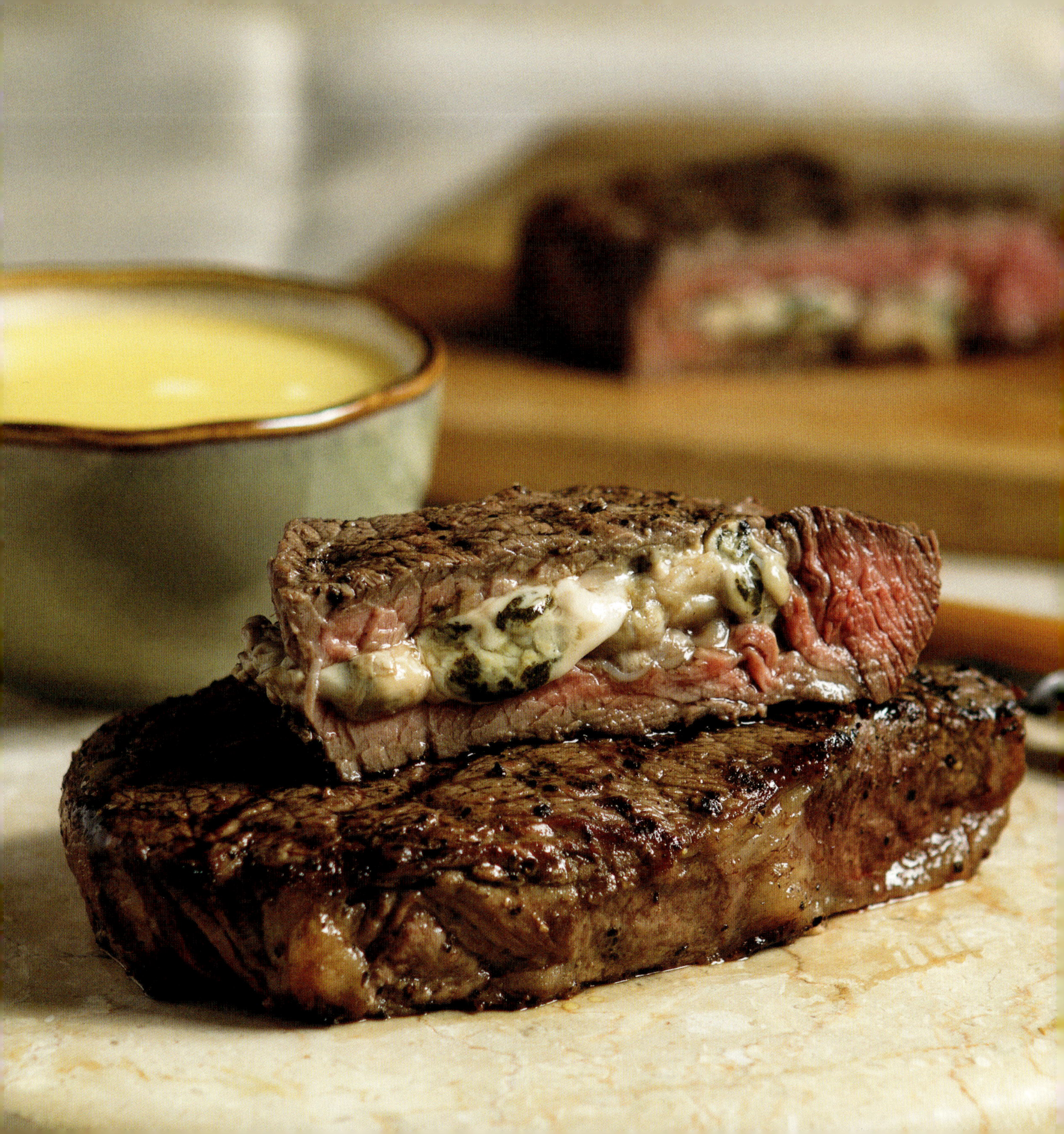

Pan Fried, Grilled, Broiled & Boiled

Carpetbag Steak

Steak and oysters are a classic combination in dishes such as steak and oyster pie and in this dish, in which a steak is stuffed with oysters before broiling or grilling.

4	sirloin steaks, 1½-inches thick
2	tablespoons Asian oyster sauce
	Freshly ground black pepper
1	dozen oysters, with their liquor
½	cup dry white wine
4	tablespoons butter, softened

Using a sharp knife, cut a long, wide pocket in the side of each steak. Brush the inside of the steaks with Asian oyster sauce and season with freshly ground black pepper. Drain oysters, reserving their liquor. Stuff 3 oysters in each steak. Thread a skewer through the side of each steak to hold oysters in place.

Broil or grill steaks to desired degree of doneness. Meanwhile, in a small saucepan, combine reserved oyster liquor and white wine, and reduce until syrupy. Whisk butter into sauce, a tablespoon at a time, until emulsified.

Place cooked steaks on serving plates and top with sauce.

Makes 4 Servings.

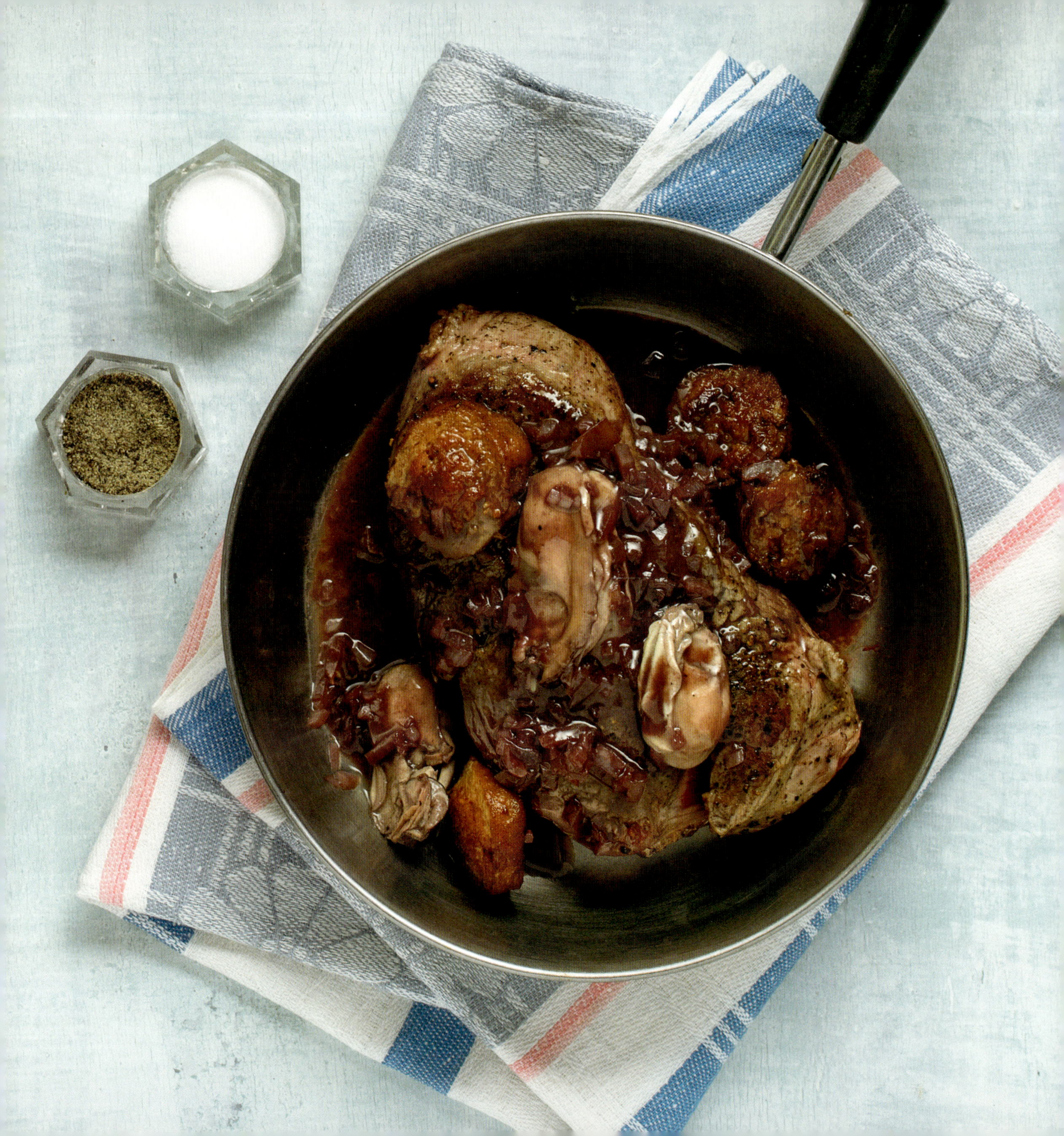

Venison with Italian Sausage & Oysters

....

If venison is not available, substitute pork loin or chicken breasts.

1	tablespoon extra-virgin olive oil
½	pound Italian sausage
4	slices venison loin
	Coarse salt & freshly ground black pepper
2	tablespoons minced shallots
½	cup red wine
1	dozen oysters, with their liquor

Heat olive oil in a heavy skillet and cook sausage on medium heat, turning frequently, until nicely browned. Cut sausage into slices and continue cooking until browned well. Remove sausage, drain on paper towels and keep warm.

Pour off fat from pan, season venison with salt and pepper and cook quickly until desired degree of doneness. Remove venison and keep warm. Add shallots and deglaze pan with red wine, scraping up any brown bits adhering to pan. Add oysters with their liquor and cook briefly until edges begin to curl. Arrange venison and sausages on warm plates and top with oysters. Cook down liquid in pan until thick and syrupy and spoon over oysters.

Makes 4 servings.

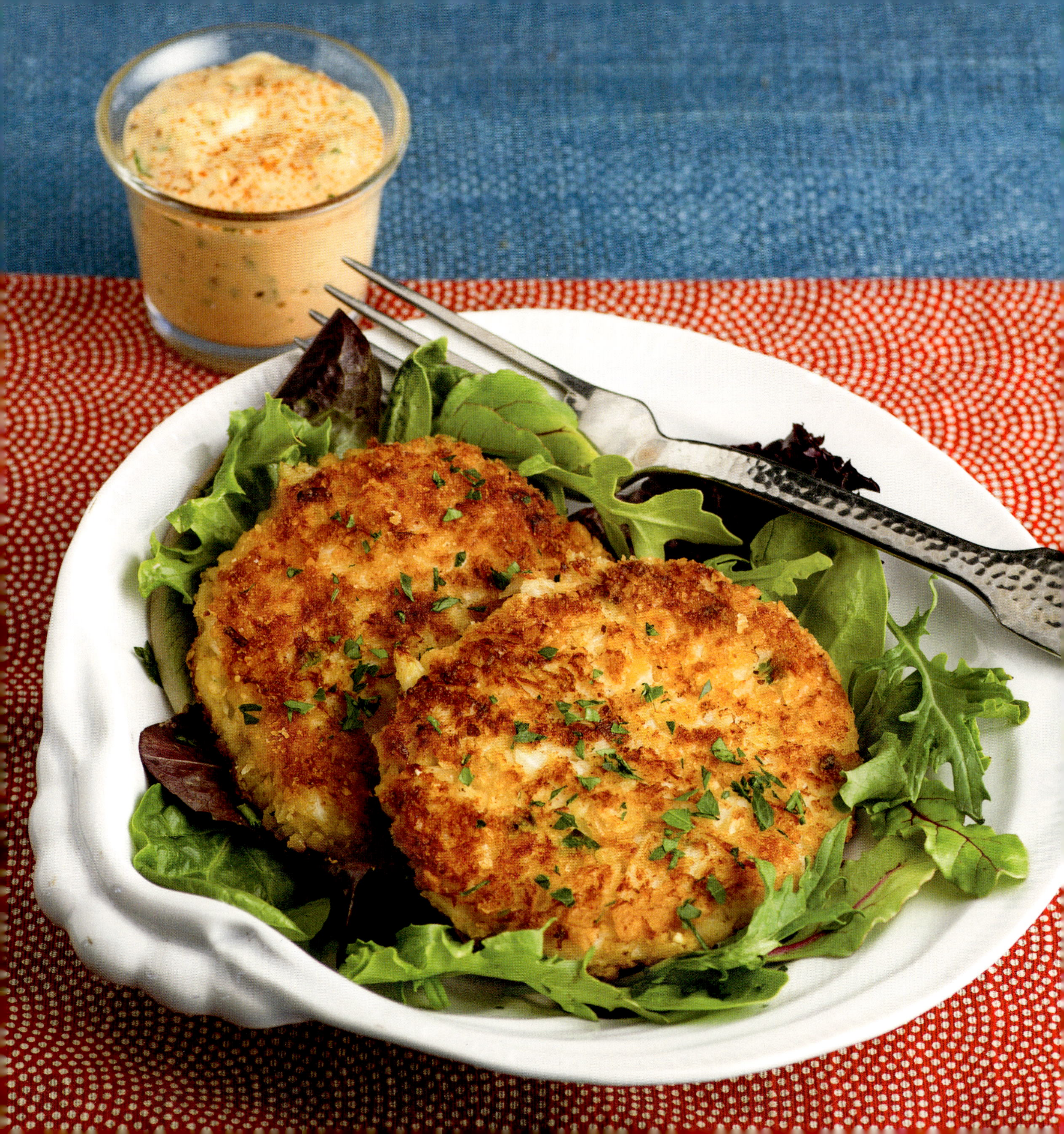

Pan Fried, Grilled, Broiled & Boiled

Shrimp Cakes

Panko, the Japanese-style breadcrumbs, create a light and crispy texture in these shrimp cakes.

1	pound boiled shrimp, peeled & deveined
6	tablespoons Panko breadcrumbs
6	tablespoons mayonnaise
	Coarse salt & freshly ground black pepper
	Hot sauce
1	tablespoon chopped parsley
½	cup all-purpose flour
	Olive or vegetable oil for frying
	Lemon wedges

In the bowl of a food processor fitted with a metal blade, pulse shrimp a few times until they are coarsely ground. Add Panko and mayonnaise and pulse to combine. Transfer mixture to a mixing bowl, season to taste with salt, pepper and hot sauce; add parsley. Form mixture into 4 cakes, dredge in flour and fry in about ¼-inch of hot oil until browned on one side, then turn and brown on the other. Drain on absorbent paper. Serve with lemon wedges.

Makes 4 servings.

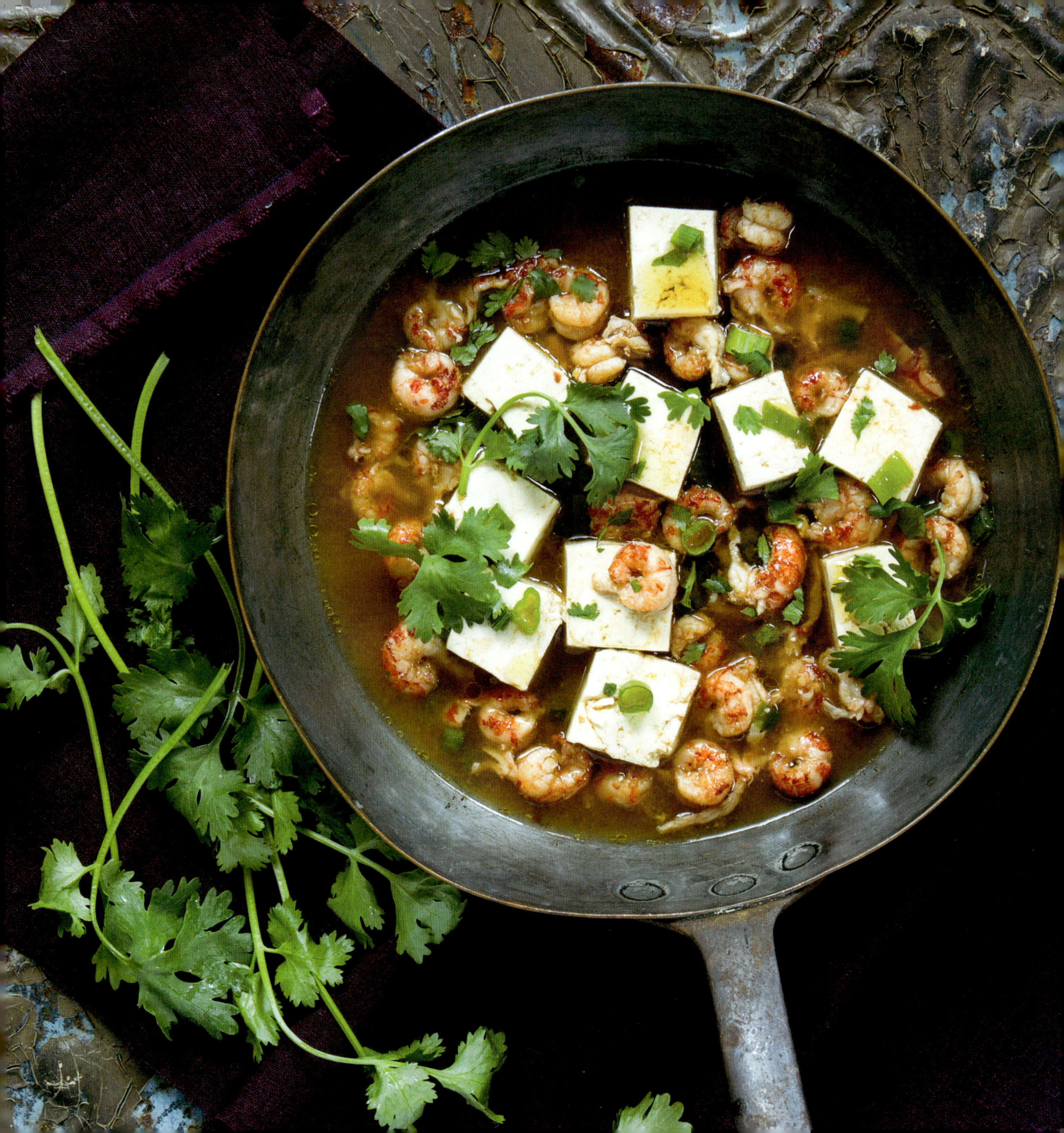

Lagniappe

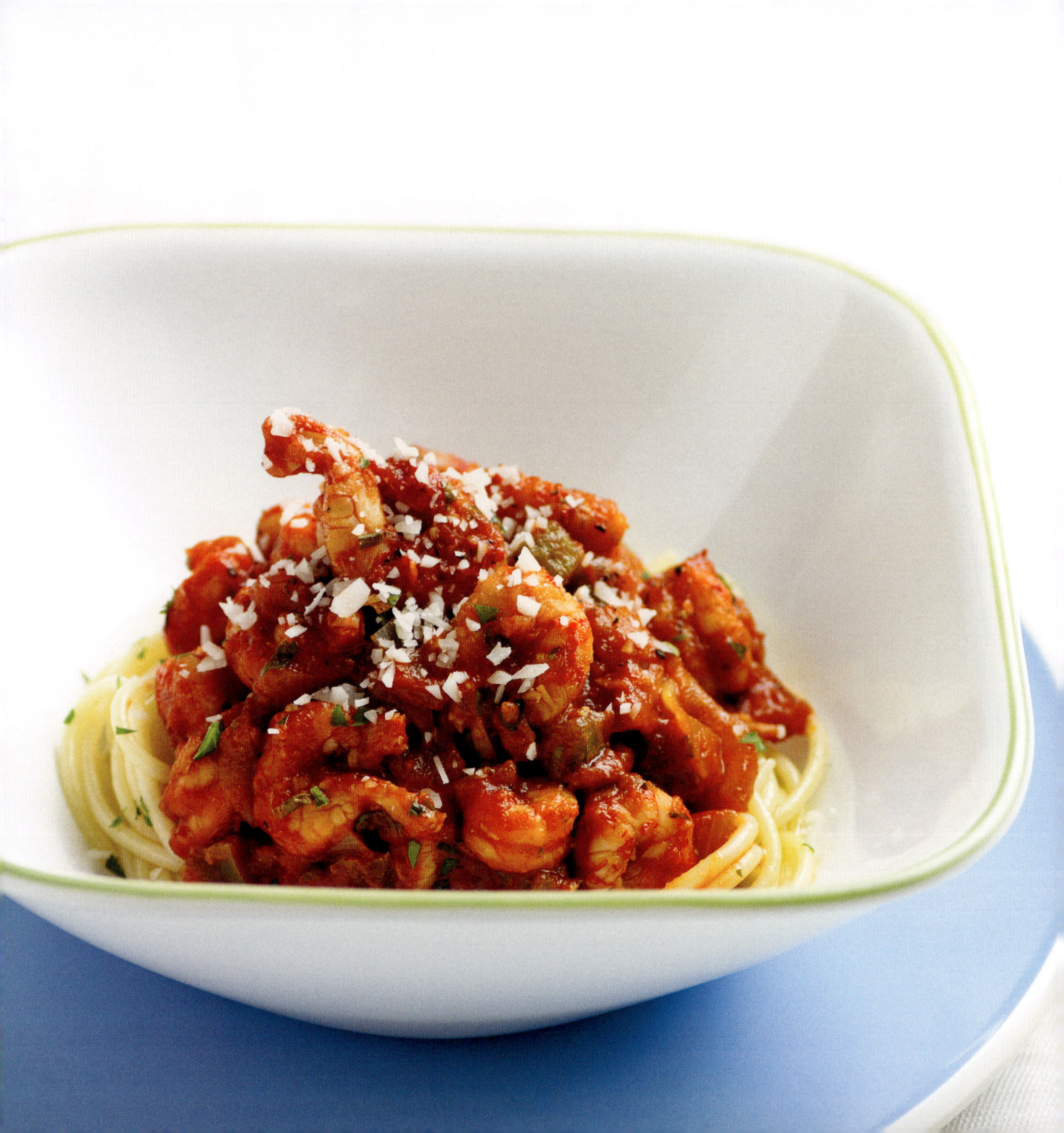

Crawfish with Red Sauce & Spaghetti

Crawfish often show up in rich cream and butter sauces that are served over pasta. This is a lighter alternative.

2	tablespoons extra-virgin olive oil
1	medium onion, chopped
1	bell pepper, chopped
4	cloves garlic, minced
1	(28 oz.) can tomato purée
½	cup chicken stock or broth
½	cup white wine
1	tablespoon cane syrup
	Coarse salt & freshly ground black pepper
	Cajun/Creole seasoning
	Hot sauce
1	pound crawfish tails
2	tablespoons chopped parsley
1	pound spaghetti
	Freshly-grated Parmesan

Heat olive oil in heavy pot, add onion, bell pepper and garlic and cook on medium heat, stirring occasionally, until softened, about 5 minutes. Add tomato purée, chicken stock or broth, wine and cane syrup. Season to taste with salt, pepper, Cajun/Creole seasoning and hot sauce. Simmer, stirring occasionally, for 30 minutes. Add crawfish and chopped parsley and simmer an additional 20 minutes. Adjust seasonings.

Meanwhile, cook spaghetti according to package instructions. Drain and transfer to serving bowl. Add sauce and toss. Serve with grated Parmesan.

Makes 4-6 servings, or more.

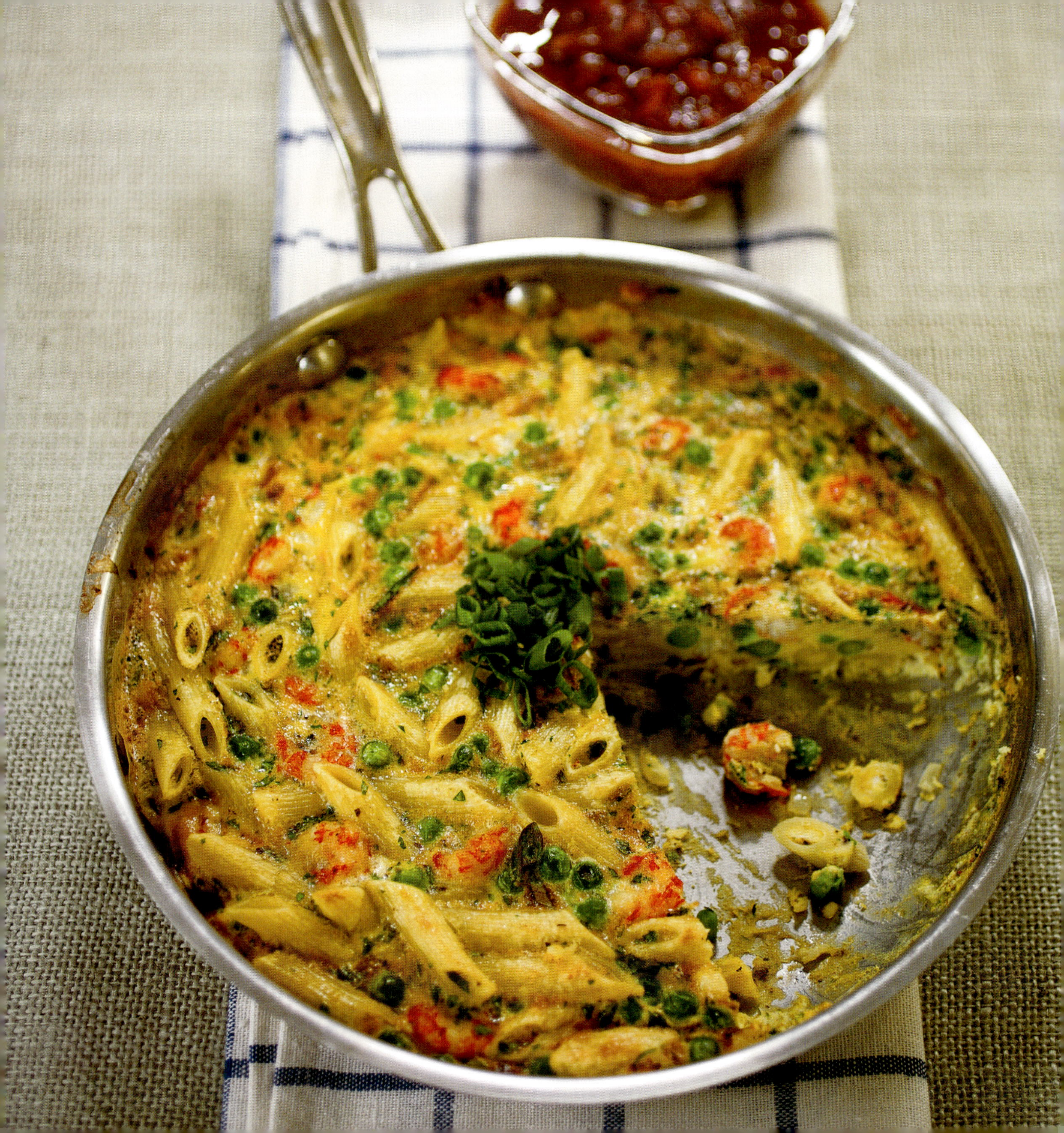

Crawfish Omelet with Penne & Green Peas

This dish is good served either hot or cold with salsa. Other types of pasta can be substituted for the penne and other vegetables, such as asparagus, can take the place of the peas.

¼	pound penne
1	cup fresh or frozen green peas
8	eggs
½	teaspoon coarse salt
	Freshly ground black pepper
1	teaspoon Cajun/Creole seasoning
½	teaspoon hot sauce
2	tablespoons chopped parsley
2	tablespoons chopped green onion tops
1	tablespoon butter
1	tablespoon extra-virgin olive oil
1	cup diced onion
½	pound crawfish tails
	Salsa

Preheat oven to 350 degrees. Cook penne in boiling salted water according to package instructions. When penne is almost cooked, add peas to the pot, then drain and refresh under cold running water. In mixing bowl, beat eggs with salt, pepper, Cajun/Creole seasoning, hot sauce, parsley and onion tops. Add penne and peas.

In an ovenproof, 9-inch skillet, cook onions in butter and oil until slightly softened, about 3 minutes. Add crawfish, stir to combine, and cook for about 2 minutes. Add egg, penne and pea mixture, and bake in preheated oven until set, about 15 minutes. Place skillet under broiler for a minute or two to brown and set top. Cut into wedges and serve with your favorite salsa.

Makes 6 servings.

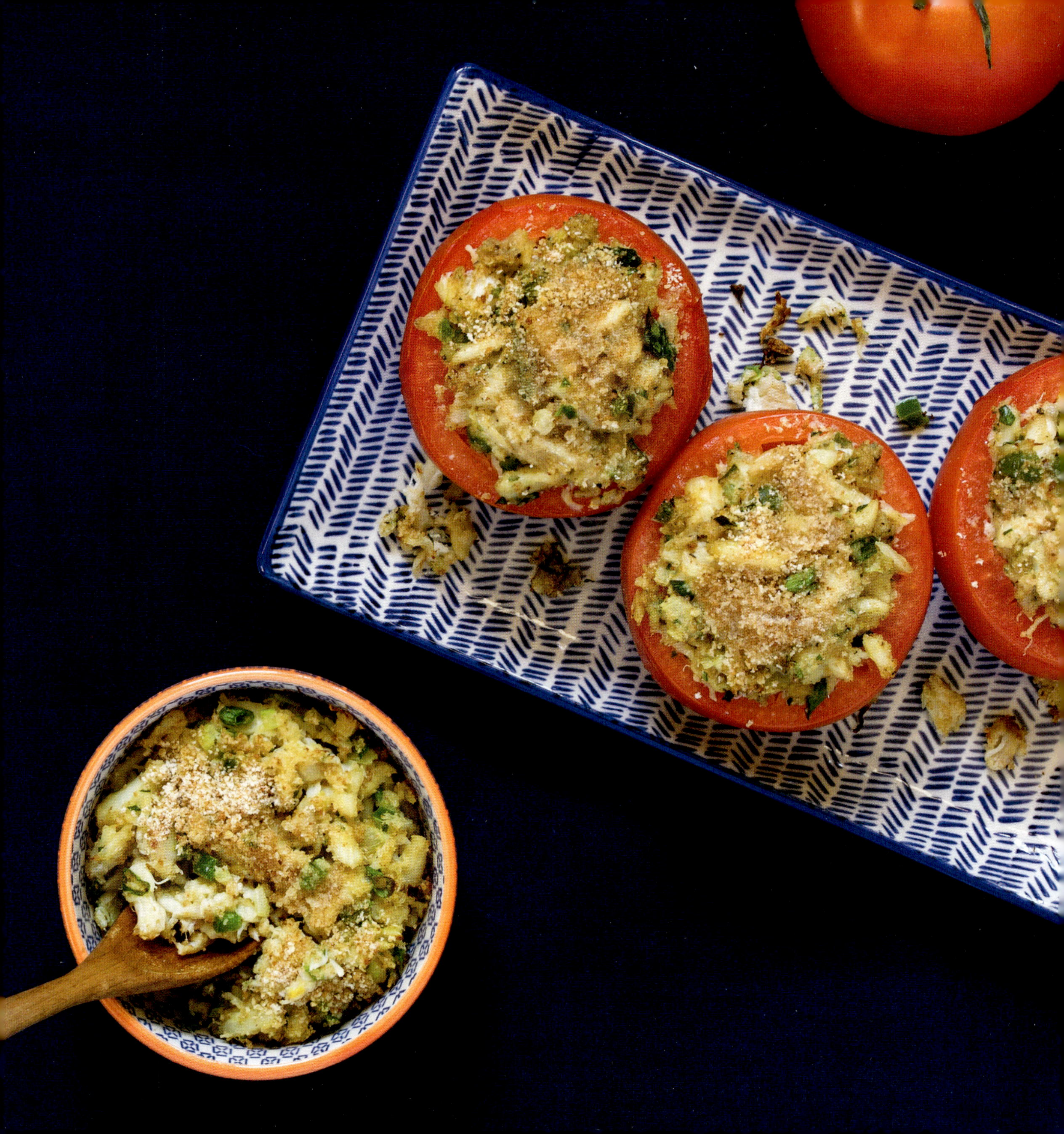

Baked Tomatoes Filled with Crabmeat

....

This crabmeat stuffing can also be baked in other vegetables, in a crab shell, in individual ramekins or used as a stuffing for fish, such as flounder.

4	*large tomatoes*
4	*tablespoons butter, plus additional for tops*
¼	*cup diced onion*
¼	*cup diced bell pepper*
¼	*cup diced celery*
½	*cup breadcrumbs, plus additional for tops*
½	*cup heavy cream*
4	*teaspoons chopped parsley*
4	*teaspoons chopped green onion tops*
1	*pound lump crabmeat, picked over*
	Coarse salt & freshly ground black pepper
	Cayenne
1	*tablespoon freshly squeezed lemon juice*

Preheat oven to 350 degrees and butter a baking dish.

Cut off tops of tomatoes; scoop out pulp and seeds with a spoon. Salt interior of tomatoes and invert on a rack to drain.

Melt butter in a frying pan, add onion, bell pepper and celery, and cook until softened, about 5 minutes. Transfer vegetables to a mixing bowl and stir in breadcrumbs. When mixture is cool, stir in cream, parsley and onion tops. Add crabmeat and toss gently. Season to taste with salt and peppers. Add lemon juice. Fill tomatoes with crabmeat mixture, mounding the tops. Sprinkle with breadcrumbs, dot with butter and bake until tops are browned, about 30 minutes.

Makes 4 servings.

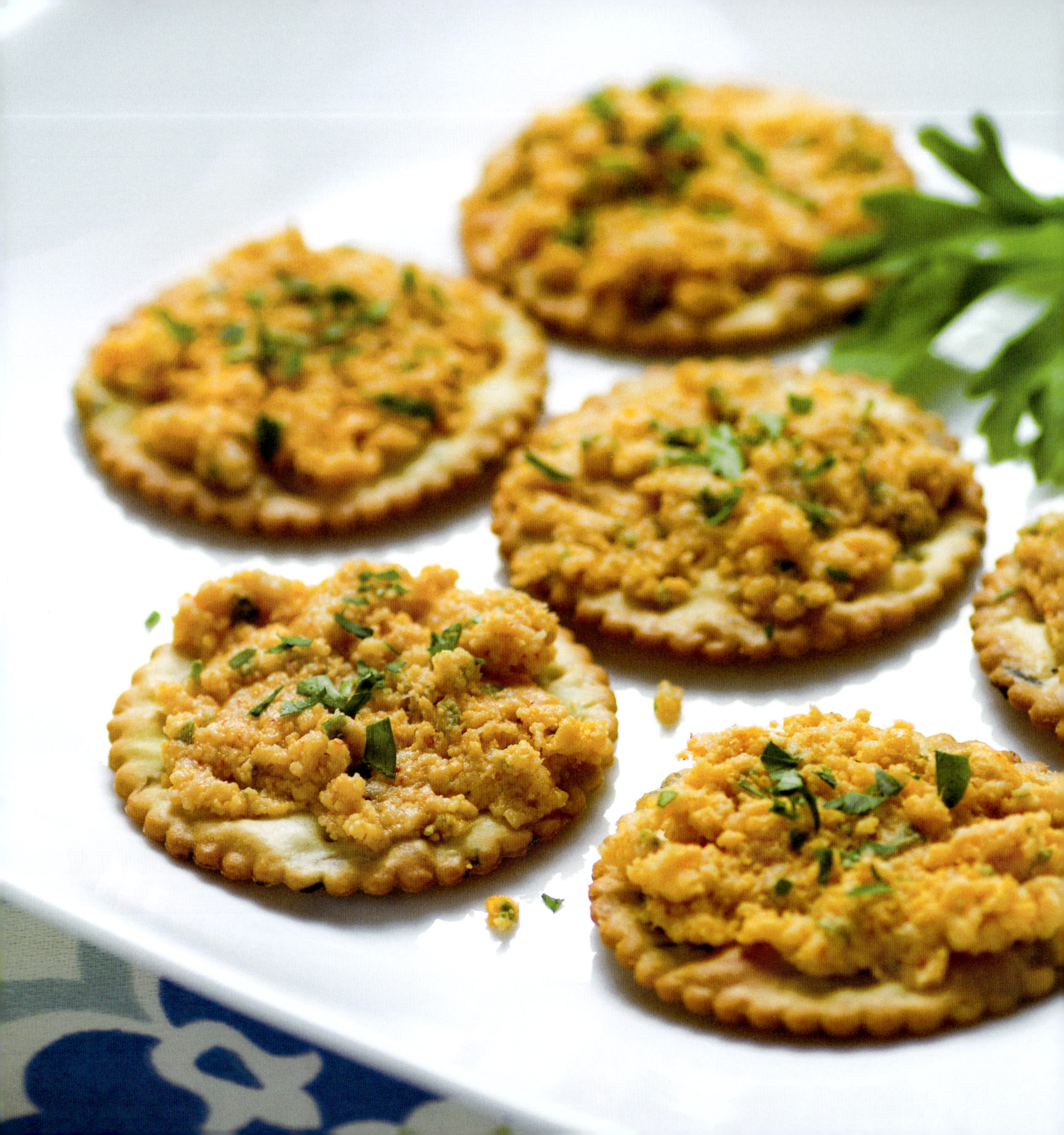

Spicy Crawfish Spread

Serve this with crackers or toasts to accompany drinks, spread a thin layer on sandwiches or use it to season baked, broiled or grilled seafood.

1½ cups cooked crawfish tails
½ cup butter, softened
4 teaspoons freshly squeezed lemon juice
Cajun/Creole seasoning
Hot sauce
1 tablespoon chopped parsley

Combine crawfish, butter and lemon juice in food processor and pulse until smooth. Season generously with Cajun/Creole seasoning and hot sauce and pulse to combine. Adjust seasoning. Add parsley and pulse to combine.

Makes about 2 cups.

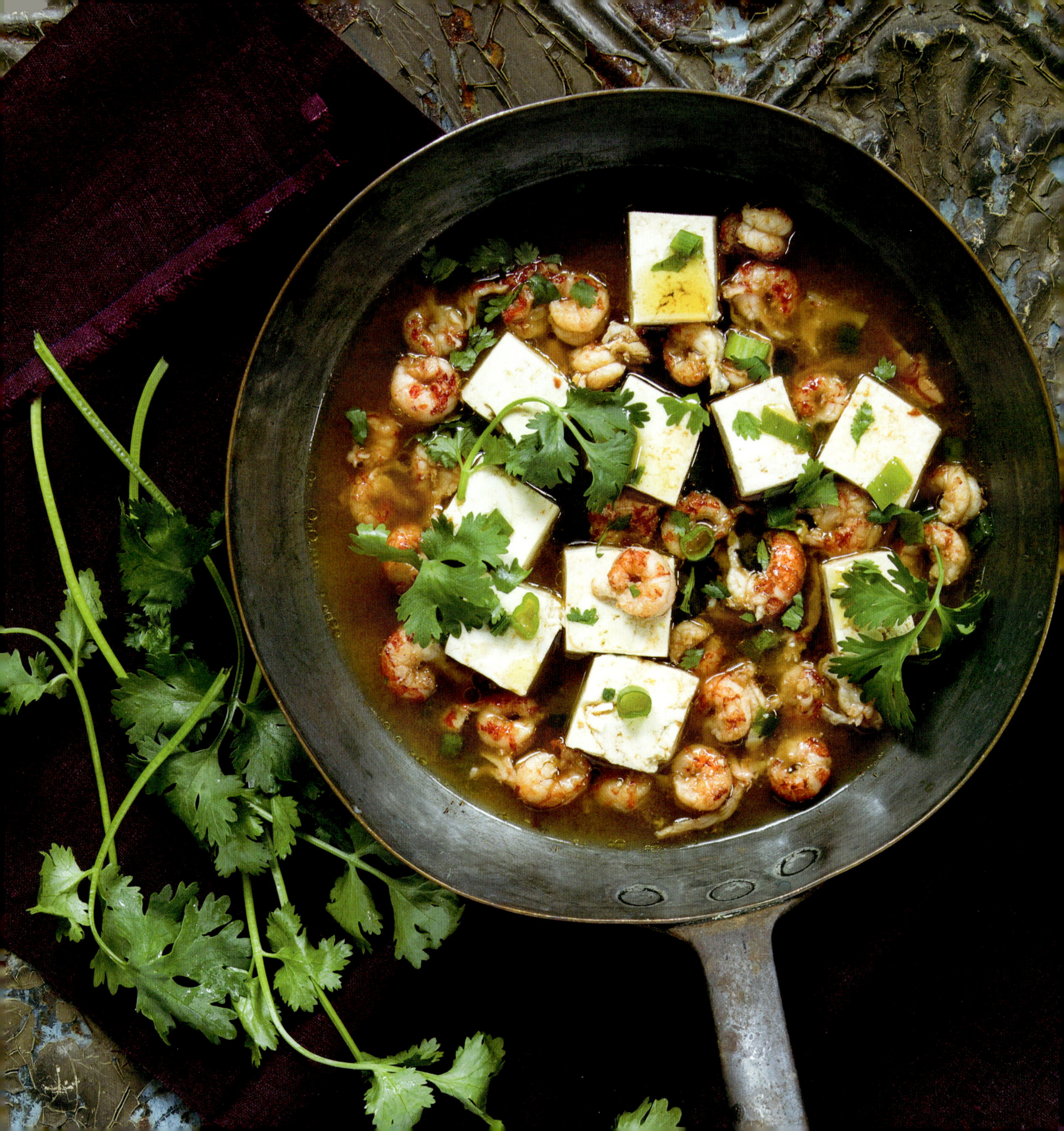

Spicy Tofu with Crawfish

This is a loose and simplified adaptation of a favorite Chinese dish, spicy bean curd with pork, bean curd being another name for tofu. It sometimes appears on menus as "Ma Po's Bean Curd" or "Family-Style Bean Curd." Tom yum paste is an all-purpose hot and sour chili paste from Thailand that is flavored with lemon grass, shallot, dried shrimp, lime, garlic and other seasonings. This dish can be prepared in less time than it takes to cook the rice.

- 1 pound firm tofu (bean curd)
- 2 cups chicken stock or broth
- 1 tablespoon tom yum paste
- 1 teaspoon soy sauce
- 1 pound cooked crawfish tails
- 2 teaspoons corn starch
- 1 tablespoon water
- ¼ cup chopped green onion tops
- 1 teaspoon sesame oil
- 2 tablespoons chopped cilantro

Cut tofu into ½-inch cubes and set aside. In a wok or large skillet, combine chicken broth, tom yum paste and soy sauce and bring to a boil. Add crawfish tails and simmer for 1 minute. Add tofu and simmer for another minute until heated through. In a small bowl, stir cornstarch into water until dissolved. Add cornstarch mixture to wok or skillet and stir carefully to avoid breaking up tofu. Add chopped green onions. Taste for seasoning and adjust as desired. Simmer until slightly thickened, then turn out into a serving bowl. Drizzle with sesame oil and sprinkle with chopped cilantro. Serve with steamed rice.

Makes about 4 servings.

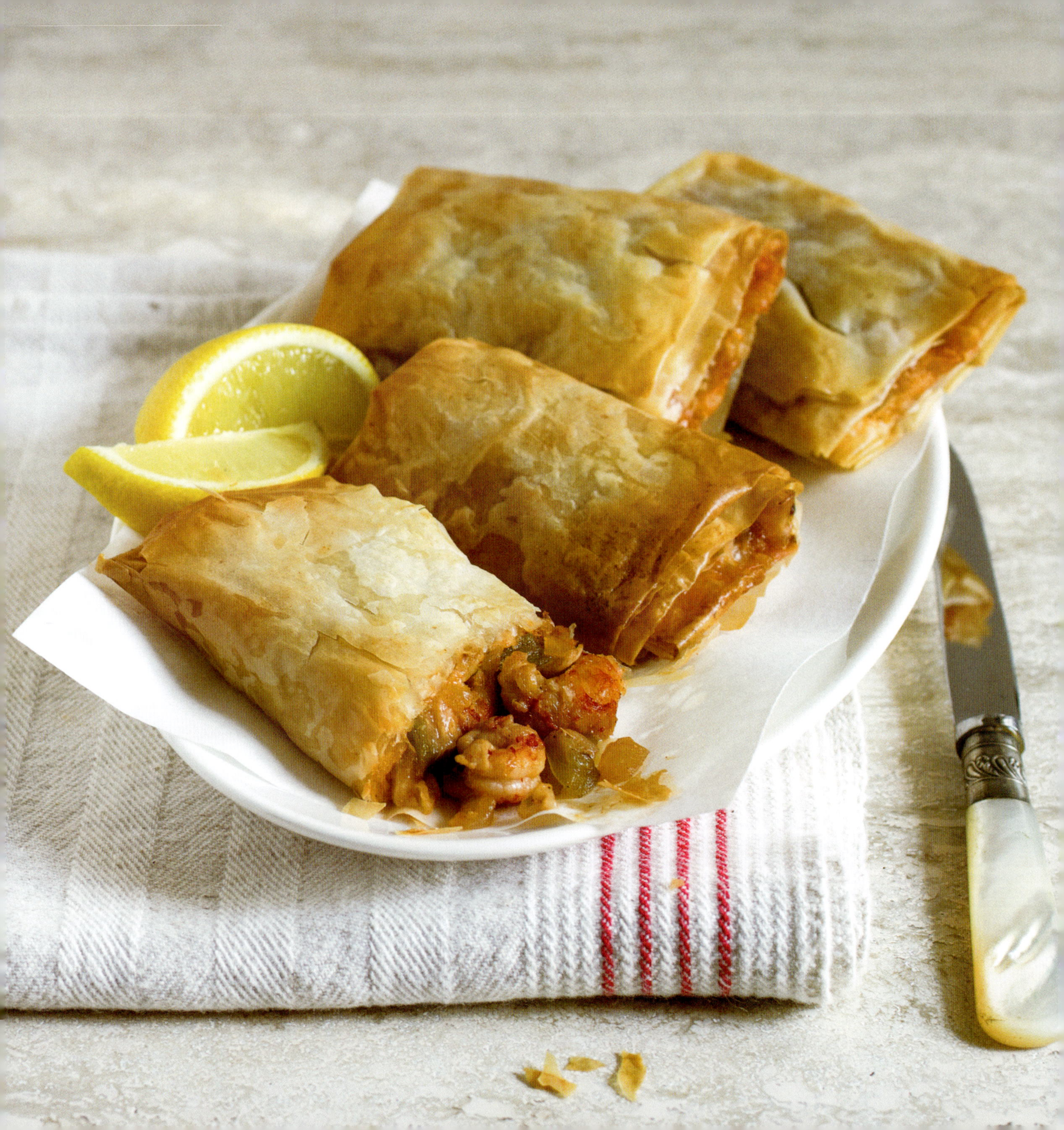

Mini Crawfish Pies

These are good either fried or baked. The filling can be made ahead of time and the pies assembled just before cooking

- 2 tablespoons olive oil
- 1 cup diced onions
- 1 cup diced bell pepper
- 6 cloves garlic, minced
- ½ pound cooked crawfish tails
- 1 tablespoon freshly squeezed lemon juice
- ½ teaspoon coarse salt
- 1 teaspoon Cajun/Creole seasoning
- 1 teaspoon smoked paprika
- ½ teaspoon freshly ground black pepper
- 2 tablespoons chopped parsley
- 2 tablespoons chopped green onion tops
- Phyllo dough (about 20 sheets)
- Vegetable oil (for frying) or
- Melted butter (for baking)

Cook onion, bell pepper and garlic in olive oil until softened about 5 minutes. Add crawfish, lemon juice, salt, Cajun/Creole seasoning, paprika and black pepper, and simmer for about 5 minutes. Add parsley and onion tops, stirring to combine. Adjust seasonings and allow mixture to cool to room temperature before proceeding.

For Frying

Place 1 tablespoon of crawfish mixture on a sheet of phyllo, centering it about 2 inches from one short end of sheet. Fold short end of phyllo over filling, then fold both sides of phyllo over filling. Continue folding toward far end of phyllo until you have a packet that measures about 1.5 inches by 3 inches. Repeat with remaining filling. Heat about a half-inch of oil in a skillet until hot, but not smoking. Working in batches, without overcrowding, quickly fry packets until brown on one side, then turn and brown on the other. Remove to absorbent paper to drain.

For Baking

Preheat oven to 350 degrees. Brush a sheet of phyllo with melted butter, then assemble packets as above, repeating until all the filling is used. As they're assembled, place each one on a lightly buttered baking sheet. Brush tops of packets with melted butter and bake in preheated oven until browned, about 10 minutes.

Makes about 20 small pies.

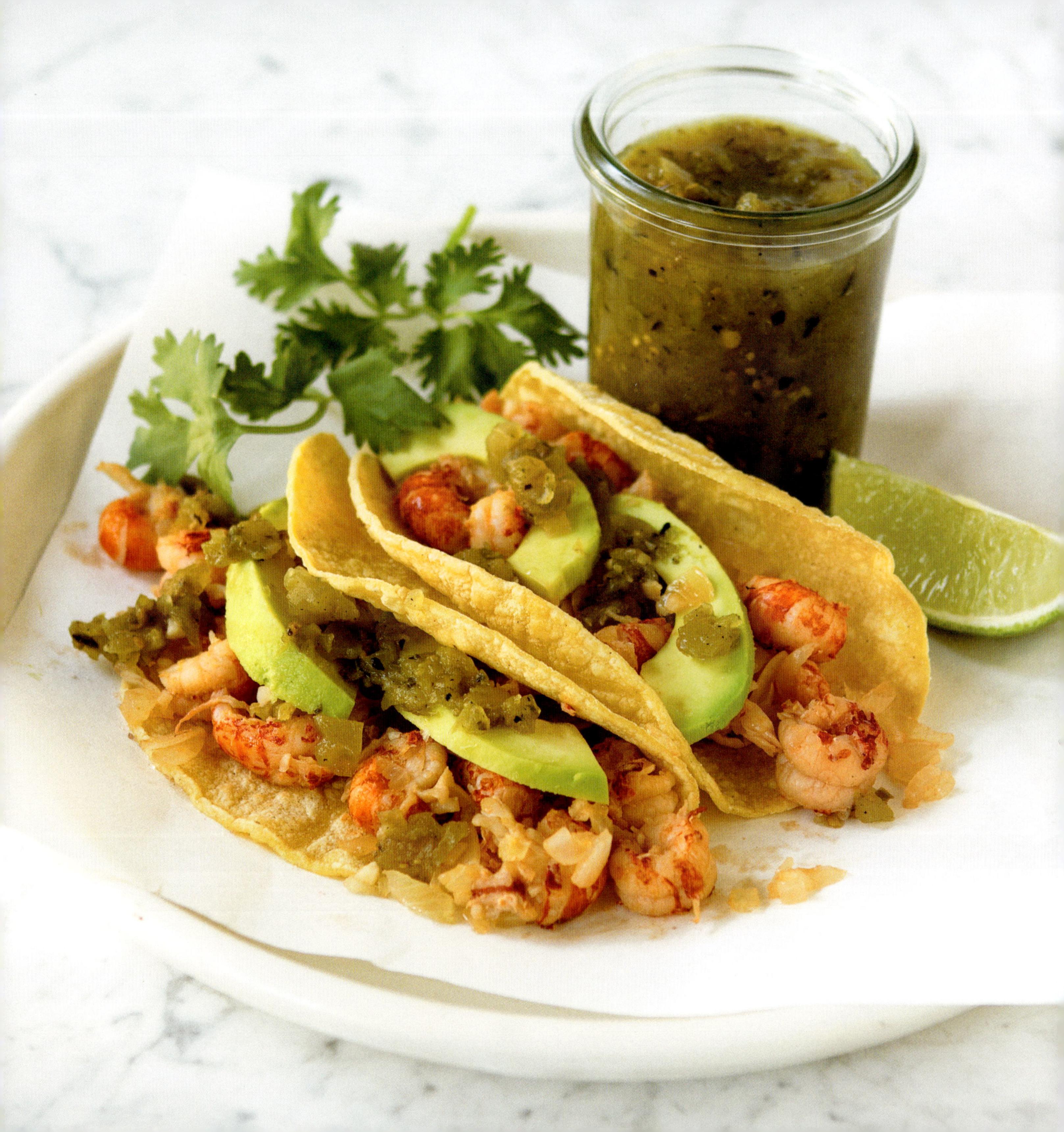

Lagniappe

Crawfish Tacos

....

These days in Louisiana, crawfish show-up in dishes from every imaginable cuisine.

SALSA

4 tomatillos

2 serrano peppers, or to taste

¼ cup loosely packed cilantro leaves

Coarse salt

TACO STUFFING

2 tablespoons extra-virgin olive oil

1 medium onion, chopped

4 cloves garlic, minced

1 pound cooked crawfish tails

Coarse salt

Freshly squeezed lime juice

TO SERVE

Corn tortillas

1–2 sliced avocados

Lime wedges

SALSA

To make salsa, remove husks from tomatillos. Wash tomatillos, place in a pan, and cover with water. Bring to a boil, reduce heat, and simmer for 5 minutes. Remove tomatillos with a slotted spoon and set aside to cool. Reserve cooking water.

Combine tomatillos, serrano peppers and cilantro in blender or food processor and purée, adding cooking water as necessary. Season with salt and process with additional peppers, if desired. Transfer salsa to a bowl.

TACO STUFFING

Heat olive oil in large skillet, add onion and cook, stirring occasionally, until onion is softened, about 5 minutes. Add garlic and cook briefly. Add crawfish and cook, stirring occasionally, for about 10 minutes. Season to taste with salt and lime juice.

TO SERVE

Heat tortillas, allowing 2 for each taco. Fill tortillas with crawfish mixture, a slice of avocado and salsa. Serve with lime wedges for each diner to use, as desired.

Makes 4 or more servings.

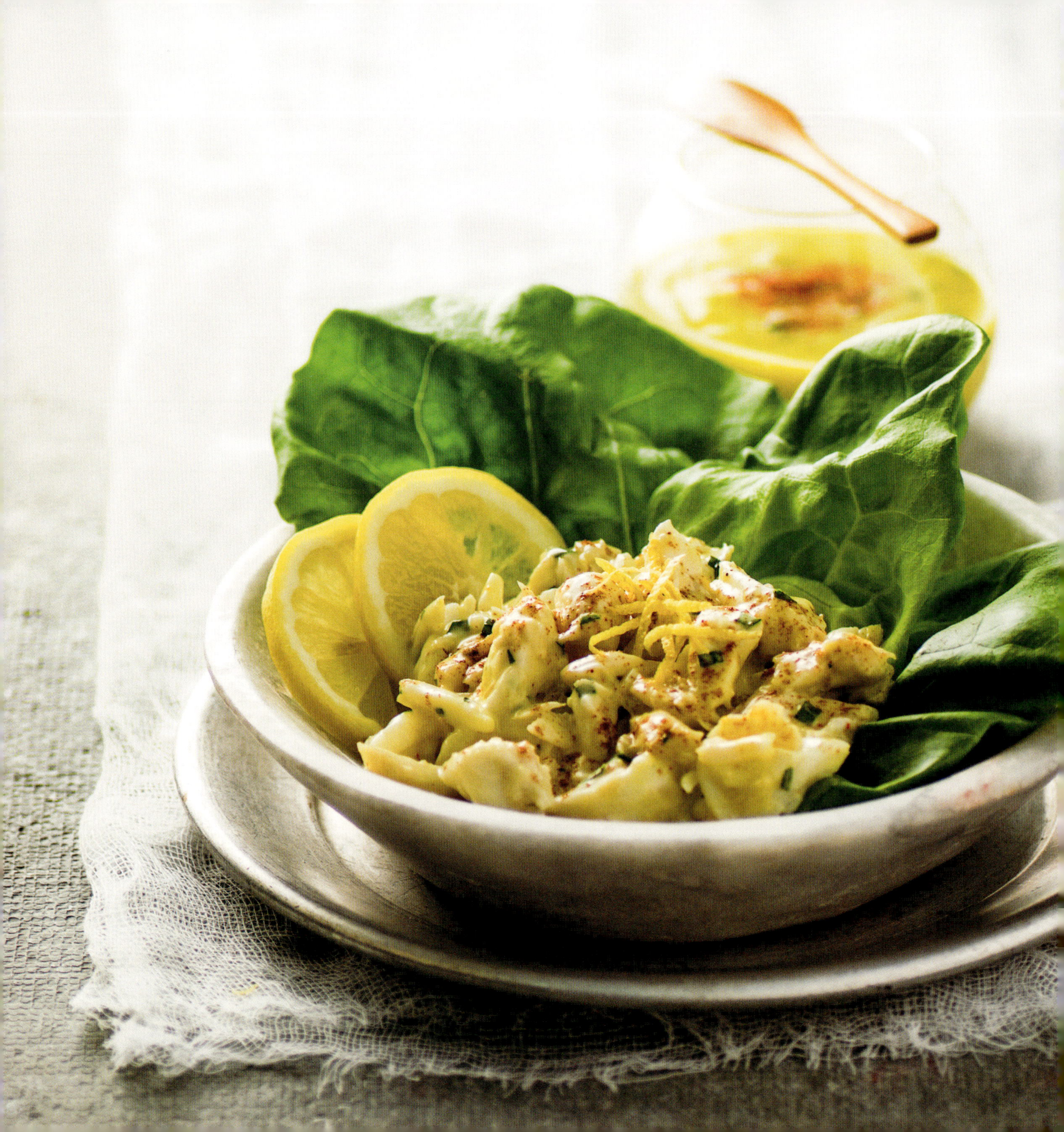

Index & Notes

Index

A
Andouille 35, 39, 47
Artichokes................................... 13, 23
Avocado.. 17, 19

B
Bok Choy 87

C
Capers 15
Courtbouillion 73
Couscous 27
Crab.....................21, 37, 89, 93, 97, 113
    Claws.. 29
    Lump.......................................13, 67
Crawfish 15, 17, 25, 55, 57, 59, 61, 63, 77, 79, 83, 87, 109, 111, 115, 117, 119, 121

D
Duck...39

E
Egg 71
    Omelet 111
    Poached 43
Eggplant..55

F
Fish
    Catfish....................................91, 95
    Gulf Fish 97
    Redfish 45
    Swordfish 51
    Trout 99
Fried Rice... 77

H
Ham 81

I
Italian Sausage 103

M
Mirliton... 83

N
Navy Bean...47

O
Okra...33, 35
Olive Salad 25
Orzo 25
Oyster........................... 37, 39, 101, 103

P
Peas 13, 111
Penne...111
Pork..69
Potato 51

Q
Quinoa..17

S
Saffron 49
Shrimp 19, 23, 27, 33, 35, 37, 41, 43, 47, 65, 67, 69, 71, 81, 105
Spaghetti...109
Steak..101

T
Tasso 43, 51, 79, 87
Tofu...117
Tomatoes...113

V
Venison..103

W
Waffle..63, 67

Notes

Notes

Notes

Stanley Dry writes the "Kitchen Gourmet" column for *Louisiana Life* magazine. Formerly senior editor of *Food & Wine* magazine, he is author of *The Essential Louisiana Cookbook* and co-author of *Gulf South*, published by Compass American Guides. His articles on food, cooking, wine, restaurants and travel have appeared in *Food & Wine*, *Travel & Leisure*, *The New York Times*, *Boston Magazine* and *Acadiana Profile*, among others. He lives in New Iberia.

Eugenia Uhl, photographer, is a native New Orleanian. Her photographs have been featured in *New Orleans Magazine*, *Southern Accents*, *Metropolitan Home*, *GQ Magazine*, *Essence*, *Travel & Leisure* and *Vegetarian Times*. Her clients include Ralph Brennan Restaurant Group, International House Hotel, Volunteers of America, Galatoire's and Tulane University.

She has completed multiple cookbooks, including *The Essential Louisiana Cookbook*, *Commander's Kitchen* for Commander's Palace and *New Orleans Home Cooking* by Dale Curry, Pelican Publishing.

42